BERNARD INGHAM'S *Yorkshire Castles*

BERNARD INGHAM'S

Yorkshire Castles

First published in Great Britain 2001 by
Dalesman Publishing Company Limited
Stable Courtyard
Broughton Hall
Skipton
North Yorkshire BD23 3AZ

Text © Bernard Ingham
Photographs © Dorothy Burrows, Jacqui Cordingley, Chris Craggs,
Collections/Yuri Lewinski, Alan Curtis, English Heritage/National
Monuments Record, Deryck Hallam, Jerry Hardman-Jones, Granville Harris,
Humber Archaeological Partnership, Roger Kilvington, Mike Kipling, Andrew
Lambert, The Landmark Trust, Ken Paver, Colin Raw, Eddie Ryle-Hodges,
David Tarn, Mike Thornton, Simon Warner, Pete Woodbridge

Cover: Bolton Castle by David Tarn

A British Cataloguing in Publication record is available for this book

ISBN 185568 193-5

Designed by Jonathan Newdick
Typeset by Barbara Allen
Colour Origination by Grasmere Digital Imaging Limited
Printed by Midas Printing (HK) Limited

*Page 2 — All that is left of the Constables' fortified
manor house known as Flamborough Castle.
Right — Scarborough's impregnable Royal castle with
800 years of military history*

Contents

Introduction

8

They jousted at Tickhill, murdered in "bloody" Pomfret, feasted fit to burst in Cawood and a Fairfax rode through his gatehouse at Steeton Hall, on the edge of the gory Vale of Towton, to claim his bride from a nunnery. That is what our ancestors got up to in their castles in an age of chivalry and treachery, pomp and privation and immense expenditure of energy. But to get to that age we need first to penetrate the mists of pre-Roman Yorkshire for that is when the story of our fortified county begins.

In going back that far I anticipate the castle by a millennium and more for the magnificent, dominating walls, towers and keeps we can still see at Richmond, Scarborough, Middleham and Conisbrough, for example, were imported from France. William the Conqueror ushered in – if he *ushered* in anything – the age of the British castle in 1066. He has left his romantic mark all over

Yorkshire but the working lives of the fortresses he and his barons built were remarkably short, although longer than the monasteries which went up with them. For most of them it was down hill all the way from 1400, assuming they were not ruinous by then. And by 1650 the Civil War did for the best of them. Parliament ordered 13 of Yorkshire's finest to be "slighted" – a curious euphemism for wrecking.

It is testimony to the yards-thick solidity of Norman castle making, if not to the cannibal-builders who later devoured their idle stones, that our landscape is still dotted and even dominated by their ruins. As Edmund Blunden put it:

Today's house makes tomorrow's road;
I knew these heaps of stone
When they were walls of grace and might,
The country's honour, art's delight.

Scarborough was in the military business until – and possibly even after – two German battleships shelled it in World War I. Some such as Bolton and Ripley (inhabited by the 29th of the line of Ingilbys) are still lived in. Hazelwood is a hotel. English Heritage bring their pasts alive for us at the incomparable Middleham as well as at Helmsley, Pickering, Scarborough, Richmond and York. Others such as Bolton, Skipton, Knaresborough, Conisbrough and Pontefract tell their stirring stories to visitors. Thanks to the forensic science of archaeologists and historians, our generations are immensely privileged in being able to look into our past with such documented clarity.

There is also a lot of our history about, even though Yorkshire is not castle-rich as compared with the Welsh Marches and Border country. Nonetheless, responding to a challenge from the publishers, I have come up with evidence of 83 Yorkshire castles and 34 fortified houses.

It is estimated there are 10,000 earthworks, cairns and barrows scattered over Yorkshire. But few of them were fortifications. Instead, many of them are the cemeteries and religious establishments of Stone, Bronze and Iron Age man and more especially of the Beaker and Urn folk who seem, from the survival of artefacts, to have concentrated in the East and North Ridings. But the experts say the wilder West Riding, the haunt of pre-historic man from the post-glacial days of the Old Stone Age, was not the wilderness I had supposed it to be. It just seems that its ground conditions don't help to preserve artefactual evidence. Excavation and aerial surveys have revealed many ritual earthwork complexes and agricultural and domestic enclosures.

These farmer-hunters were not a bellicose lot. They seemed to lead peaceful pastoral lives for century after century without much evidence of mayhem or defences against it. They escaped the southern pressures of land hunger and in the East Riding quietly absorbed the Hallstatts from Holland and the horsemen from the Seine – the Parisii. But then came Julius Caesar to invade the vast territory of Brigantia, taking in Durham and Lancashire as well as Yorkshire's broad acres. The Parisii of the East Riding were soon Romanised. The Brigantes were less tractable, if you ignore Queen Cartimandua, Yorkshire's first collaborator.

There were small Iron Age hill forts before

this, perhaps one of the earliest at Knapton, north east of Malton, and later examples at Castlesteads in the far north-west near the border with County Durham, and at Eston Nab, overlooking the Tees. The fort on top of Ingleborough, one of Yorkshire's "Three Peaks", also pre-dates the Romans as well as that at Almondbury, Huddersfield, now the site of a Victorian tower. But it may well be that the invasion triggered the construction of other Brigantian fortifications such as at Wincobank in Sheffield and at Castle Stead ring between Bingley and Haworth, the literary shrine of the Brontës.

The huge fortification at Stanwick, north of Richmond, was central to Venutius' resistance from AD69-74 until Petillius Cerialis, conqueror of Boadecia, broke him and his Brigantian forces who promptly melted into the hills.

Like all occupying forces, the Romans looked to their own protection. Yorkshire has a plethora of Roman military remains along the roads they established for all time. In the old West Riding, remains of forts are to be found, for example, at Elslack and Long Preston, south west and north west of Skipton; Ilkley (Olicana); at Sheffield in the Don Valley below Wincobank; and at Newton Kyme, north west of Tadcaster.

In the North and East Ridings they protected their territory with signal stations, on the coast most notably on the site of Scarborough Castle, and at the mouth of the Stainmore Pass to Carlisle at Bowes. Bainbridge (Virosidum), one of the best investigated upland forts, Malton (Derventio) and Brough (Petuaria), commanding the Humber, were also important. At Cawthorn, north of Pickering, they seem to have recycled an Iron Age fort which was later used by Anglo-Saxons and even Vikings. One theory is that Cawthorn was a Roman training camp where they learned defensive skills and probably how to build Hadrian's Wall. All these were controlled from York (Eboracum) and segments of the walls of the 9th Legion's fortified camp can still be seen there.

The Romans abandoned their British empire after about 350 years and Yorkshire descended into the Dark Ages. The Vikings arrived in waves to do what came naturally to them – to rape, pillage, set fire to churches and settle. But they didn't leave much evidence of their military presence apart from two things: sculptures of war lords with their weapons and Dane's Dyke, a mighty ditch cutting off Flamborough Head from the rest of Yorkshire, although nobody seems sure who actually dug it. It would be nice to record the remains of the sort of Scandinavian halls from which Beowulf was called upon by King Hrothgar to banish the monster Grendel. Unfortunately, one of the best Anglo-Saxon/Scandinavian occupational sites at Ribblehead did not have one. The nearest approach is a 13th-century version found by excavators at Huttons Ambo, south west of Malton.

And then came the Conqueror. Within two years York had two wooden castles on mottes or mounds either side of the Ouse. Their sites can be seen to this day and on one stands a successor, the imposing Clifford's Tower. Both had to be replaced within a year when the natives revolted. To teach Yorkshire a lesson, William embarked on his "Harrying of the North" which slaughtered thousands and laid waste to vast tracts of the county. Yorkshire was out on its feet for decades.

William and the Norman barons on whom he bestowed territory wisely took the precaution of securing their domains and protecting themselves from what was left of the surly, resentful indigenous population, not to mention the Scottish marauders to the North. They embarked upon a major castle-building programme which involved a massive amount of earth shifting and timber felling. Their classic fortress, replacing the old Anglo-Saxon ditches and palisades, was a wooden tower on top of a mound with a courtyard, all surrounded by a fortified ditch reached through a gatehouse via a drawbridge.

In their first flush of castle construction – that is, in the generation after 1066 – they first dominated the county towns – in this case, York – and then proclaimed their iron hand with forts elsewhere. Uniquely for his time, Alan the Red of Brittany seems to have constructed Richmond castle in stone from the outset. Standing on a cliff above the Swale, he enclosed his courtyards behind massive stone walls with towers. He also set his living quarters apart from the gatehouse, on which was eventually built the tower we see today. Scolland's Hall, as they are called, is one of the earliest examples of Norman domestic architecture. Richmond is also one of Yorkshire's best preserved castles even though it was one of the first to be built. It had curiously little strategic value.

I would feel happier if I could set out the chronological development of Yorkshire's stock of castles. Unfortunately, in common with the rest of England, many of them have no written history. The provenance of a quarter of the 82 Yorkshire castles listed in this book is not known. Only about 700 of the 1,700 in England and Wales have any visible masonry, though some may be buried in the remaining earthworks. Against this background, Yorkshire seems relatively well off for visible remains, as our photographs demonstrate. But that does not solve the problem of listing them in age order.

In any case, the ruins we see today are not usually those of the original castle. In the early days they were built in wood only to be replaced later by magnificent stone edifices. Of those pictured in this book, Pickering, Sandal and Tickhill seem to qualify for the first wave. The second phase, dating loosely from 1100, produced a magnificent crop in Knaresborough, Cropton, Crayke, Conisbrough, Scarborough, Helmsley, Skipton, Ravensworth, Whorlton, majestic Middleham, Bowes and possibly Scargill, both now in County Durham but in Yorkshire until 1974, and Hazelwood.

A tremendous burst of renewal or rebuilding of existing castles followed in the 14th century – of Knaresborough, Middleham, Mulgrave, Pickering, Pontefract, Ravensworth and Skipton. It also brought much private enterprise, as distinct from royal, castle building. In Yorkshire it created Harewood, Cawood (for the Archbishops of York), and four "private" castles built around 1380 to an imposing four square, four corner-towered template – Bolton, Sheriff Hutton, Danby and Wressle.

Later we saw the rise of the private pele tower house, of the kind familiar in the Borders, to protect families of note from the Scottish raiders. It might be argued that Bowes was the mighty early example since it is just a tower. Gilling Castle, absorbed into Ampleforth's preparatory school, and West Ayton, near Scarborough, are good examples of pele towers. We also acquired fortified houses for the same purpose. Markenfield Hall, just south of Ripon, is the outstanding example in the North of a medieval moated farm house. Nappa Hall, stronghold of the Metcalfes, near Askrigg, and Slingsby and Spofforth Castles are also notable. There are also a couple of examples of church towers – at Bedale and Leathley, near Otley – which served the same defensive purpose for congregations pestered by Scottish marauders.

There is much argument over what is a castle and what is a fortified house. There are those who would claim that Bolton – and presumably its mates Sheriff Hutton, Wressle and Danby –

Ripley Castle's walled garden

are fortified houses. They have a point. The castle went through various stages of development from wooden castle on a motte, with bailey and ditch, to their stone version, some round, buttressed keeps and splayed bases as at Conisbrough to thwart mining, then castles without keeps but with elaborate surrounding curtain walls with towers and offices built inside the ranges of wall such as at Middleham, to four-square Bolton with an inner courtyard and rooms in every range.

There was one guiding principle: an attempt to reconcile defensive purpose with domestic comfort. Bolton became fit for a queen for Mary Queen of Scots was incarcerated there. Indeed, along with its mates, it represents the zenith of Yorkshire military architecture before gracious domestic living took over and the end of the Civil War brought from 1650 what can only be described as an epidemic of grand house building. In a mere 50 years we moved from castles which Cromwell finally knocked about a bit to the baroque glory of Castle Howard.

I have drawn maps of all the castles for which I have found evidence in search of a strategic pattern. If it shows one thing, it is that the West and East Ridings are not castle country. The 100-mile long Yorkshire coast was left largely unprotected apart from Scarborough and the encasement of Hull within a long-since disappeared brick wall. The Pennine wall to the West was presumably seen as sufficient deterrent provided Stainmore (Bowes), Swaledale (Richmond) and the Aire Gap (Skipton) were controlled. True. York, which sometimes served as England's capital, was eventually pretty well surrounded by forts. But Yorkshire's real castle country is the North Riding. And that tells you where, once the Normans had lost their fear of the Anglo-Saxons and Scandinavian invasion, the real danger came from: the Scots.

There was one other menace: the nobles who built the castles. They were a threat to the king and themselves. The Percys, Mowbrays, Nevilles, Scropes, Cliffords, Warennes, de Lacys and Talbots were a troublesome lot. They gave weak kings such as John and Henry III a terrible run-around. Sometimes they even aligned themselves with the Scots. Henry II tried to curb their power and actually appropriated the "adulterine" Scarborough Castle from William le Gros who had put it up without licence. The nobles' rivalries came to a head in the Wars of the Roses. Yorkshire was anything but solid for the Yorkist cause but fortunately most of the population was spared this medieval power feud.

Perhaps because of their quarrelsome natures – and because they were their prestigious seats – the castle declined more slowly in Yorkshire than elsewhere. John Leland, in his chronicle of castles around 1540, gave a good report – and some glowing ones – for more Yorkshire castles than he recorded in ruin. But the writing was on the wall in his account, for example, of Pickering: "The castle walls and towers be meetly well, the lodgings in the inner court that be of timber be in ruin…"

It is difficult to argue that gunpowder rendered the castle obsolete when Skipton, Sandal, Helmsley, Knaresborough, Scarborough, Pontefract (the last to surrender in England) and even the minimally protected Bolton could only be starved out by Parliament. But the Civil War brought the curtain down on the great show our castles had staged for 450 years. Parliament ordered Bolton, Cawood, Crayke, Helmsley, Knaresborough, Middleham, Mulgrave, Pontefract, Sandal, Sheffield, Skipton, Tickhill and Wressle to be made untenable – 13 in all.

Monarchs frequently bestrode the battlements of Yorkshire's castles. They hunted and fought over the county, spent thousands on royal castles such as Pickering and Scarborough and no doubt despaired of the barons holding others. Middleham competes with Pontefract for the title the "Windsor of the North" – court, palace and castle – and was undoubtedly Richard III's favourite. Cawood was an Archbishop's palace and administrative and political hothouse. Bolton, Wressle and Sheriff Hutton were sumptuous and sophisticated houses in their hey day. The rest of this book seeks to encapsulate their romantic past. It is a stirring tale which inspired the likes of Wordsworth and Sir Walter Scott to literary acclaim.

Castles and Fortified Houses in Yorkshire

Castles

This book is primarily about Yorkshire's castles and fortified houses. Defensive works left by Ancient Britons, Romans and Vikings are too numerous to specify, assuming it were possible to list them all. But you can be detailed, if not entirely exhaustive, about the ancient county's castles and fortified houses. This book may well fuel the fire over what is a castle and what is a fortified house. If so, it is in character. I have never knowingly left the embers of an argument unfanned.

The following lists deal first with castles and then fortified houses for which evidence is recorded. It identifies in *italic* those featured in this book. The old, traditional riding in which each was built is also indicated by ER, NR or WR.

Aldbrough, ER, on the Holderness coast 12 miles east of Hull; mounds near Bewick Hall are the only remains of a moated castle of the Norman de Melsas (c1150-1377). Leland, in his *Itinerary* in Henry VIII's time, described it as "great ruins".

Aughton, ER, six miles north east of Selby; earthworks of motte and bailey castle on the approach to the church across the track from the moated site of the manor house of the Askes. Robert Aske, of Aughton, was executed for leading the Pilgrimage of Grace, a protest against the Dissolution of the Monasteries, in 1536.

Bardsey, WR, north east of Leeds, there is the motte of a castle north of the church which began as a Saxon shrine.

Barwick-in-Elmet, WR, east of Leeds, an historic place where the Saxon Council used to meet;

vast earthworks which could have been a Brigantes camp or a Celtic stockade and evidence of a Norman motte.

Bolsterstone, WR, just south of Stocksbridge, near Sheffield, east of the church the remains of the gatehouse of a castle built about 1250.

Bradfield, WR, three miles south of Bolsterstone in the high Pennines, evidence of a motte and bailey castle.

Burton-in-Lonsdale, WR, a motte with two baileys on private land but reputedly royal property in the Conqueror's day; the Mowbrays had it taken away from them in 1322 after apparently holding it against Edward II's will.

Cottingham, ER, North Hull, Baynard's Castle had a brief life from late 12th century and was ruinous by 1360. Outer ditch and bank destroyed, but inner ditch surrounds a mound on which The Manor House (17th century) stands. King John was entertained here by William de Stuteville and Edward I by the Wakes. Heiress of Wakes in 1349 was Joan Plantagenet who married the Black Prince.

Bolton, NR, in Wensleydale, the great redoubt which balances military with domestic requirements and where Mary Queen of Scots was held prisoner.

Buttercrambe, NR, north east of Stamford Bridge, hillock remains of motte and bailey castle in the grounds of Aldby Park.

Bowes, now in County Durham but formerly in NR, guarded the Stainmore Pass.

Breckenbrough, NR, site on the banks of the Wiske near Sion House at Kirby Wiske, five miles north west of Thirsk, home of the Lascelles for centuries

Bronsholm, ER, at Swine, six miles north east of Hull, only remains are a shapeless earthwork with ditch and bank; said to have been built before 1200 and crenellated without a licence in 1352.

Burstwick, ER, once the seat of Holderness government, east of Hedon, moat and earthworks of a castle used as a base by Edward I and Edward III for their campaigns against the Scots in the late 13th and early 14th centuries.

Robert the Bruce's queen was imprisoned here from 1306-8.

Carlton, NR, near Wensley, remains of a conical motte.

Castleton, NR, deep in the North York Moors and high in the Esk Valley 15 miles west of Whitby; Norman horseshoe-shaped motte, but no bailey; where stood the stone castle of the Yorkshire Bruces from c1160; north wall said to have been 13ft thick.

Catterick, NR, traces of what some claim is a Norman motte and bailey castle, north of the church; the churchyard is assumed to have been the site of the bailey; others think it could be a prehistoric barrow.

Catterick, NR, on the Swale to the south east of the village, Norman motte and bailey castle.

Cave, ER, at South Cave originally built by the Normans beside a Roman road just north of the old Roman Humber river crossing at Brough; now a hotel.

Cawood, WR, once splendid castle-palace of the Archbishops of York, four miles north west of Selby.

Conisbrough, WR, the castle and splendid keep between Rotherham and Doncaster which inspired Sir Walter Scott's Ivanhoe.

Cotherstone, County Durham but formerly in NR, to the north west of Barnard Castle. Motte but no bailey; records of a licence to crenellate in 1200-01.

Crayke, NR, two miles north east of Easingwold, a fortified hill top for 1,400 years and site of a castle for centuries associated with the Bishops of Durham.

Cropton, NR, four miles north west of Pickering on the southern edge of the North York Moors, remains of Robert de Stuteville's motte and bailey castle.

Danby, NR, a mile east of Castleton in the Esk Valley 14 miles west of Whitby lie the ruins of the Latimers' early 14th-century castle.

Drax, WR, five miles south east of Selby, Normans had a castle here but it has gone along with the priory near the Ouse, apart from a moat and earthworks.

Foss, NR, one of two ancient castles at Mulgrave, north west of Whitby (see Old Mulgrave, below); a wooden motte and bailey castle built by Nigel Fossard which lasted at most 130 years when it was replaced around 1200 by Old Mulgrave on a nearby site.

Harewood, WR, between Leeds and Harrogate, ruin of the single bastion redoubt of the Aldburghs from 1367 within the Harewood estate.

Harlsey, NR, in the Wiske valley west of the A19 just across from Cleveland Tontine, rectangular enclosure with a 30ft ditch on three sides and some evidence of the basement of a keep.

Hazelwood, WR, just south of Tadcaster overlooking the bloody Vale of Towton, home of the Vavasours for 800 years; now a hotel.

Hedon, ER, Leland, in his 16th-century *Itinerary*, found only "tokens of a pile or castle".

Helmsley, NR, the magnificent ruins of the second wave of Norman fortifications back on to the North York Moors.

Hinderskelfe, NR, the predecessor on a different site of Castle Howard, owned by the Howards from 1571; noted by Leland in the mid-16th century as "no ample thing"; re-built in 1683 and destroyed by fire ten years later. Castle Howard followed.

Hornby, NR, 14th-century castle of the St Quintins four miles north west of Bedale and much altered over the centuries.

Hutton Conyers, NR, mutilated remains of a Norman motte and bailey castle within concentric ditches and banks and two courts.

Kildale, NR, four miles east of Stokesley at the northern end of the North York Moors, an oval mound of a Percy motte and bailey castle west of the church.

Killerby, NR, two miles north west of Kirkby Fleetham, in Swaledale south east of Catterick, a ruin in Leland's *Itinerary*; the moat and a little walling of an early 13th-century castle remain; so do the bailey and bits of a motte of its predecessor on the marshes of the Swale.

Kilton, NR, ruined stronghold of the Thwengs, hidden away in the woods a mile south west of Loftus in NE Yorkshire.

Kimberworth, WR, evidence of a small motte and bailey castle close to the Manor House on the edge of Rotherham.

Kirkby Malzeard, WR, Norman castle of the Mowbrays of which only rubble and heaps of stone remain.

Kirkbymoorside, NR, only the moat and a small portion of wall can be traced of a de Stuteville castle on a degraded mound on Vivers Hill, north of the church.

Kirk Leavington, NR, just south of Yarm, a Norman motte surrounded by a ditch above the River Leven.

Knaresborough, WR, ruins of a royal castle on the cliffs above the Nidd founded 30 years after the Battle of Hastings.

Laughton-en-le-Morthen, WR about five miles south east of Rotherham the site of a Norman motte and bailey castle by the church, which was begun by the Saxons.

Leconfield, ER, the Percys, Earls of Northumberland, were granted a licence to crenellate in 1308. It had a high embattled brick wall, with brick towers at each corner and a two-storey gatehouse. One of the principal residences of Henry "the Magnificent", 5th Earl, in the early 16th century. Demolished 1608-9 and lots of it removed to Wressle Castle. Moated area survives.

Malton, NR, the Norman castle built on the site of the Roman camp, Derventio has gone (apart from the gatehouse integrated into a 17th-century gateway). Leland reported it "hath been large, as it appearith by the ruin. There is at this time (16th century) no habitation on it but a mean house for a farmer". It was followed around 1600 by a manor house which has also largely vanished.

Mexborough, WR, castle mound part of public gardens.

Middleham, NR, arguably Yorkshire's finest castle

ruin, perhaps most entitled to the title "The Windsor of the North" in the days of that "glorious son of York", Richard III.

Mount Ferrant, ER, a mile south west of Birdsall, near Malton, Only the earthworks of a Norman castle built by the Fossards remain on a spur of the Wolds escarpment; It had a short life, being destroyed about 1150. Leland's *Itinerary* in the 16th century reported it "now clearly defaced and bushes grow where it stood".

Newton Kyme, WR, two miles north west of Tadcaster, a fragment of the wall of a castle in the gardens of Newton Hall.

Northallerton, NR, west of the church, Norman motte and bailey castle, some say built by William the Conqueror. Leland reported: "2 flight shots wnw from it [the Bishop of Durham's palace] be ditches where the castle of Alverton sometime stood. No part of the walls thereof now appearith". Bailey visible and motte cut through by railway.

Old Mulgrave, NR, stone replacement of Foss Castle (see above) around 1200 on a new site 700 yards away at Mulgrave, near Whitby, ruinous by 1309. What was left of it by the Parliamentarians was incorporated in New Mulgrave Castle's landscaped grounds.

Pickering, NR, magnificent ruins which began as William the Conqueror's first royal castle and visited by most English kings between 1100 and 1400.

Pickhill, NR, just east of the A1, five miles west of Thirsk, square mound, surrounded by a 60ft-wide ditch, of a motte and bailey castle built by the Constables just west of the church.

Pontefract, WR, "thou bloody prison" as one of its victims described it. Ruins of one of the noblest Plantagenet castles in the North near the confluence of the Calder and Aire with an awesome history.

Ravensworth, NR, another castle which inspired Sir Walter Scott. The fragments remaining on the bleak site near the County Durham border between Richmond and Barnard Castle take us back to the FitzHughs who ruled these wild parts in the 12-16th centuries.

Richmond, NR, the magnificently preserved keep set on top of the early Norman gatehouse is one of the most imposing in the country and there are ruins of one of the earliest halls in English castles.

Ripley, WR, north of Harrogate just off the road to Ripon, home of the Ingilbys for 700 years and now occupied by the 29th of the line; 15th-century gatehouse built to keep the Scots out, opens on to the courtyard and the original tower block remains.

Roos, ER, only the earthworks remain of the medieval castle of the Roos near the Holderness coast just north west of Withernsea. Robert Roos fought for Richard the Lionheart and witnessed the signing of the Magna Carta.

Roxby, NR, a mile west of Thornton Dale, only mounds remain of a castle which was the home of the Chomleys; one, Sir Richard, known as the Great Black Knight of the North in Elizabeth's time, was apparently famous for his hospitality.

Sandal, WR, local castle at Wakefield, eight miles from Pontefract, of circular stone construction like the de Warennes' other castle at Conisbrough.

Scarborough, NR, the Plantagenets poured money into the development and maintenance of this great bastion which dominates the spa from its headland. Its working life extended over 800 years until it was shelled during World War I.

Scargill, now in County Durham but formerly in NR, now only the gatehouse ruins remain of the important 14th-century castle which also moved Sir Walter Scott.

Sheffield, WR, what little bit remains of the Earl of Shrewsbury's fortress is now subsumed in the city's Castle Market; Mary Queen of Scots was imprisoned there for 14 years. It was destroyed at the end of the Civil War.

Sheriff Hutton, NR, celebrated home of the Nevilles from which the first Tudor queen of England emerged. Remains we see today are of the second built there on the lines of Bolton. The site of the first is at the east end of the village.

Sigston, NR, only a mound and ditch remain where the Sigstons' wooden castle stood at Kirby

Sigston, three miles east of Northallerton.

Skelton, NR, the present modern castle stands in Cleveland where the Bruces built their stronghold inside a very wide moat; the Fauconbergs made it new in 1330.

Skipsea, ER, one of Yorkshire's earliest castles which had a motte on an island in the old mere and was reached by a causeway across the water; the mere and all bar the earthworks have gone.

Skipton, WR, one of the best preserved castles in Britain, at the top of the market town's main street, thanks to a remarkable woman, the last of the line of the Lancastrian Cliffords.

Snape, NR, another Neville fortress near Bedale from which Catherine Parr emerged to become Henry VIII's last wife, and, by luck and good management, his widow.

Tadcaster, WR, Leland reported in the 16th century: "A mighty great hill, ditches and garth of this castle on Wharfe be yet seen"; no longer, but it is said that some of its stone is in the old bridge which spans the river.

Thirsk, NR, only traces of one of the Mowbrays' castles built by Roger de Mowbray; he made the mistake of being part of a failed rebellion against Henry II who demolished his fortress. Leland says "At Thirsk was a great castle".

Thorne, WR, Leland reported "a pretty pile or castelet well ditched" now long forgotten, even by the most assiduous chroniclers.

Tickhill, WR, at the southern extremity of Yorkshire on the site of a Brigantian settlement, Roger de Busli's great castle became one of the few places licensed for jousting.

Topcliffe, NR, five miles north east of Ripon, Maiden's Bower, as the original English home of the Percys is known; motte, said to have only ever had a wooden castle on it, built soon after 1071 and strengthened in 1174. Motte to the east and bailey to the west, both with ditches.

Upsall, NR, today's modern castle was originally a 14th-century redoubt of the mighty Scropes and there is a tall tale told about the building of the medieval castle.

Wetherby, WR, traces of a castle to the south of

the market place; it rose above the Wharfe near the six-arch bridge.

Whorlton, NR, only the gatehouse and tunnel-vaulted cellars remain of the castle built in this ill-fated place on the north-western edge of the North York Moors by the de Meynells.

Wressle, ER, the most important castle ruin in East Yorkshire in the grand style of Bolton, Sheriff Hutton and Danby – a palace fort of the powerful Percys.

Yafforth, NR, only the motte of a castle remains on Howe Hill west of the River Wiske a couple of miles north west of Northallerton.

York, William the Conqueror built two castles on either side of the River Ouse. Not much remains of Baile Hill but Clifford's Tower is a famous sight and curiously bears the name of a Lancastrian hung in chains from it in 1322.

Fortified Houses

Aske Hall, NR, near Richmond, a 15th-century pele tower standing behind the east wing of what appears to be a magnificent Georgian mansion, home of the Marquess of Zetland

Barden Tower, WR, above Bolton Abbey in Wharfedale; supposedly built as a Clifford hunting lodge; three storeys high; rebuilt in 1485 by the Shepherd Lord who emerged illiterate from the hills where he had been hidden as a boy after the Wars of the Roses to claim his inheritance – Skipton Castle.

Bolton-upon-Swale Old Hall, NR, just east of Catterick, three-storey pele tower with a two-storey wing later attached to it.

Burton Agnes Old Hall, ER, between Driffield and Bridlington, a three-floor, medieval delight which is neither castellated nor regarded as a fortified house but was built 1170-80 in classic fortified style with an arch leading into a vaulted stone undercroft with the great hall above.

Colburn Hall, NR, hall of a fortified manor house, once home of the D'Arcys, three miles south east of Richmond.

Cowton Castle, NR, three-storey oblong tower house, with two corner towers, on the hillside overlooking the marshes at South Cowton in the Wiske Valley near Scotch Corner.

Danby Hall, NR, east of Middleham, near Jervaulx Abbey, embattled pele tower of the 14 or 15th century with ranges of buildings connected to it.

Flamborough, ER, earthworks and a chalk fragment of the tower of the Constable family's fortified manor house for which a licence to crenellate was granted in 1351. Leland, in his *Itinerary*, said "Flamburg is now taken rather for a maner place then a castle".

Farnhill House, WR, between Keighley and Skipton, with four square embattled turrets, described by Nikolaus Pevsner as "an interesting relic of an early 14th-century house".

Gilling Castle, NR, the preparatory school of Ampleforth, the main block of which is a 14th-century pele tower built as a defence against hit and run Scots.

Halsham, ER, half way between Hedon and Withernsea, earthworks marking the site of a manor house, occupied by the Constables from the late 12th century until they moved to Burton Constable in the late 16th century.

Heath Old Hall, WR, near Wakefield, built between 1584-95, remains of a roughly square Elizabethan hall with small inner courtyard, battlemented turrets and parapet. It is what is now described as "an Elizabethan prodigy house" that is, the first of its type.

Hipswell Hall, NR, in the village believed to be the birthplace of John Wycliffe, near Richmond; hall's tower porch is dated 1596 and the front is castellated.

Hooton Pagnell Hall, WR, six miles north west of Doncaster, has a 14th-century gatehouse with carriage and pedestrian entrances and a lot of

19th-century castellation.

Howden Manor House, ER, a stopping place owned by the Bishops of Durham; the 14th-century great hall and two-storey battlemented porch survives.

Hutton Colswain Hall, NR, excavations on the site at Huttons Ambo just south west of Malton found evidence of two successive crudely-built halls, circa 13th century, with Scandinavian features.

Low Burton Hall, NR, at Masham, regarded as an interesting fortified house of the 13th century, once the home of the Scropes and garrisoned by the King in the Civil War.

Markenfield Hall, WR, three miles south of Ripon, the finest example of a medieval moated farmhouse in the North, a working farm and home of the Lords Grantley, dates back to 1310.

Marmion Tower, NR, at West Tanfield, south east of Masham stands the only surviving bit of the Marmion family's stronghold – the embattled gatehouse.

Mortham Tower, NR, built by the Rokebys on the old Yorkshire/Durham border and features in Sir Walter Scott's poem *Rokeby*.

Nappa Hall, NR, near Askrigg, the fortified manor house built in 1459, with two towers of different height linked by a single storey hall; a fine example of how a family of note – in this case the Metcalfes – sought to protect themselves from Scottish marauders.

Paull Holme Tower, ER, a striking Lincolnshire-style fort in brick downstream of Hull which is the only remaining part of the Holme family's fortified house.

Riccall Manor House, ER, between Selby and York, medieval home of the prebend largely rebuilt in 1869, but at one corner there is a three-storey tower with turret in late 15th-century brick.

Sheffield Manor, WR, remains of the Earl of Shrewsbury's home, built in the 15th century and dismantled in 1706, including the three-storeyed Turret House, a sort of summer house with turrets.

Sinnington Hall, NR, four miles west of Pickering stands a barn north of the church which Nikolaus Pevsner, the architectural authority, said "must once have been the great hall of a manor house or castle".

Slingsby Castle, NR, in Ryedale, north west of Malton, never completed and never a home but originally a magnificent fortified Elizabethan house with high walls, corner turrets and vaulted cellars; it began life as a Mowbray castle in the Conqueror's day.

Spofforth Castle, WR, generally regarded as a fortified house between Wetherby and Harrogate which the powerful Percy family kept losing and winning back until Parliamentarians wrecked it.

Steeton Hall, WR, four miles north of Ferrybridge, surviving gatehouse, dating from 1360 of the medieval hall of the famous Fairfaxes through which one of them rode to claim a bride from a nunnery.

Thornhill Manor House, WR, just south of Dewsbury, ruins of the manor house of the Saviles east of the church surrounded by a moat.

Walburn Hall, NR, at Downholme, four miles south west of Richmond, an Elizabethan fortified house with an embattled wall, wall walk and flagged courtyard.

Weaverthorpe, ER, half way between Malton and Bridlington, the churchyard extends on to the site of a 12-14th-century fortified manor house; chalk foundations excavated in 1960 uncovered evidence of two large rectangular buildings; the manor house was enclosed by a bank.

Well Hall, NR, just east of Masham, with evidence from its vaulted undercroft to features in its fabric of the original 13th-century fortified manor house.

West Ayton, NR, south west of Scarborough, three-storey stone tower built in the 14th century in Northumberland style, whence its owner came, but really more for domestic than defensive purposes on the site of a former manorial centre.

Wilton, NR, the mighty Bulmers preceded William the Conqueror and were lords of Wilton until the 16th century. Sir Ralph de Bulmer was given a licence in 1330 to convert his manor house at Wilton into a castle.

Ingleborough

Our journey through the history of ancient fortified Yorkshire begins on the roof of the county. On top of Ingleborough, to be precise. Here 2,372ft up, sitting on the millstone grit cap worn by one of Yorkshire's three celebrated limestone peaks, lies the highest hill fort in England. It pre-dates the Romans and is thought to be the result of increased tension in society which caused farming communities to come defensively together. The earliest Dalesmen retreated into the clouds when danger threatened.

They built a 13ft-thick wall in compartments in the shape of a pear around the 15-acre summit plateau. Sadly, where it is not eroded, it has all too often plundered by the thousands of fell walkers who like to add their own stone to one of the summit cairns. It seems likely that the entrance was at the most vulnerable north-east corner. It was no mean fort. Indeed, given Ingleborough's majestic natural ramparts as well as the perimeter wall, it was probably impregnable in the short-term. But with rain the only form of water supply it was vulnerable to siege. And yet you can also see the circular footings of at least 20 stone huts suggesting it was something more than a mere bolt hole. Common sense tells you it was a summer retreat. Who would live on the top of Ingleborough in winter, even in the more benign climate of Roman Britain?

There is no evidence that the fort was ever beseiged. In fact, there are those who suggest that when the Romans put down Venutius' revolt at Stanwick near Richmond in AD74 the defeated Brigantes melted away to Ingleborough, their original stronghold, "there to vanish into the mists of the Celtic twilight".

Stanwick

30

From the heights at Ingleborough we descend to Stanwick, north of Richmond, to the largest hill fort in Britain by a long chalk. It lies just north of the A66, which follows the Roman road over the Stainmore pass into Cumbria, near the village of Forcett. The massive earthworks cover 850 acres and a tiny part of them under the guardianship of English Heritage are open to the public. This is the area considered of outstanding significance by Sir Mortimer Wheeler when he excavated it in 1951-52.

Researchers now think that Stanwick was much more than a hill fort – indeed, a major pre-Norman market centre and seat of Brigantian power. Under the Wheeler theory, the fortifications were built by the Brigantes who ruled the North of England when the Romans invaded. At their heart is an oval enclosure called the Tofts. They were then vastly increased in size during the 1st century AD. This tremendous earth shifting and stone-walling is thought to have been the work of Venutius, the anti-Roman husband of that great collaborator, Queen Cartimandua. She was quite a girl. After divorcing Venutius, she rubbed salt into his wounds by cohabiting with his armour bearer. He rose in open revolt in AD69 and Cartimandua was forced to seek Roman protection.

The Romans could not put up with these rebels and guerrillas in their midst. In AD71 Emperor Vespasian ordered his governor of Britain, Petillius Cerialis, who had honed his skills against Boadecia, to bring them to heel. It took him four years and his campaign is thought to have ended with the capture of Stanwick as the remnants of Venutius's forces took to the hills.

Castle Hill, Almondbury

Nearly 1,000ft up on the Pennines south east of Huddersfield stands a landmark which viewed from a distance lends this large worsted town a feeling of Camelot. It is the Victoria Tower at Almondbury named after the Queen whose diamond jubilee it commemorated in 1897. The tower may be nobbut a spring chicken in the great sweep of history covered by this book but, as the museum within shows, it occupies a site which was home to tribesmen as long ago as 2150BC. It also became an important redoubt of the Brigantes.

They went to a lot of trouble to fortify this eight-acre hill top around 300BC. First they cut a ditch and built a rampart across the south end. Then they extended the rampart right around the summit and finally they enclosed the lot with a huge outer rampart. But it was anything but impregnable and the anti-Roman faction of the Brigantes had to fall back on Stanwick, near Richmond, when the Romans overran it.

Another thousand years went by before the Norman de Lacys, rewarded with vast lands around Huddersfield by William the Conquerer, built a stone keep, protected by the original Celtic ramparts, on spoil ripped up from the western half of the Iron Age site. It became a hunting lodge before Henry III knocked it down. Since then it's been a beacon hill to warn of the Armada and Napoleon, a site for large political and religious meetings and almost anything else you can think of from prize, dog and cock fighting to Sunday School picnics. This just shows you what can happen to Iron Age forts.

Multangular Tower, York

Yorkshire is teeming with Roman remains and, if the forts of the legions are not two a penny, there is plenty of evidence of them in all three of the old ridings. But none is quite so well preserved as in Eboracum, as York used to be called. This was the Northern command HQ next to what became one of the highest ranking civilian towns in the entire province of Britannia. Indeed, two Roman emperors died visiting this northern outpost of their empire in AD211 and 306.

York owes its existence to the 9th Legion of the Roman Army which established its 50-acre fortress on the north-east bank of the Ouse in AD71. The 6th Legion took over around 120 and remained to the end of the Roman period. The civilian settlement grew outside the southern defences and across the Ouse and was eventually given the title colonia to denote its importance.

You can get some idea of the fortress by walking along the modern city's medieval walls from Aldwark via Monk Bar to Bootham Bar and through the King's Manor to Museum Gardens. This covers about half the perimeter of the Roman fortress for today's walls follow the line of its northern defences. And in the Museum Gardens you find the Multangular Tower with the neat, regular stonework of the Romans surmounted by the larger and less regular upper fabric which was added to create medieval defences – a sort of recycling of fortifications.

Cawthorn Roman Camps

If you want to see where, one theory has it, Roman soldiers practised making forts in the 2nd century AD you should take a look at the Cawthorn Roman camps – there are four – on top of an escarpment just inside the North York Moors National Park off the A170 north of Pickering. They lie side by side running east-west and the two most westerly are open to the public, thanks to the National Park Committee which bought the site in 1983.

They are also close to the Roman road across the moors connecting the Derventio fort (now Malton) with the coast. It seems that the camps were built in two stages and that the most westerly and most easterly were added. The westerly of the two in the middle is coffin-shaped and provides evidence of the systematic training which professional Roman soldiers underwent. Perhaps this is where some of Hadrian's men learned their wall-building techniques further north.

The easterly of the two middle camps is the most impressive with its 10ft rampart broken by entrances on each side of its square covering 6.5 acres. Within there were turf huts with streets and in the south-eastern corner a Bronze Age barrow which was used as a reviewing platform for the commander. This is evidence that the site has a longer, complex history. You can walk through the double-ditched most westerly square fort from the westerly entrance passing the central site of the principia building. Just sit there and you may hear the centurion's barked orders echoing down the centuries – in a sort of Latin, of course.

Dane's Dyke

And now behold a mystery. It is a tremendous earthwork which cuts off Flamborough Head, that great white snout of the chalk Wolds projecting into the North Sea. It is 2.5 miles long, runs north-south and faces west – ie the rest of Yorkshire – with banks up to 18ft high on either side of a 60ft-wide ditch on average 26ft deep. It is by any standards a formidable defensive system. But who built it to protect the handful of square miles of headland which has come to be known as Little Denmark?

Was it an Iron Age or even Stone Age rampart? Well, Arthur Mee, that great chronicler of Britain, had no doubt it was there centuries before the Danes arrived to colonise Yorkshire in the Dark Ages. Rawnsley and Singleton, in their *A History of Yorkshire* make it Iron Age. Jane Hatcher, the distinguished architectural historian of Yorkshire, rather begs to differ. So does Nikolaus Pevsner, the great chronicler of Britain's buildings. Both make it Anglo-Saxon. And Pevsner's archaeological collaborator, J B Whitwell, is inclined to link it with the brief encampment of King Ida there in the 6th century.

Whoever built it must have felt singularly insecure. Fancy going to all that trouble to defend a tiny corner – or invader's toehold – of Yorkshire? You can get the best views of this mighty feat of early navvies where the Dyke is crossed by the B1229 and B1255 roads out of Flamborough village.

39

Richmond

Count Alan the Red of Brittany was quick off the mark after William the Conqueror had set about commanding his new nation by building castles in the major centres such as York. This soldier and friend of the Queen was granted many of the forfeited estates of the old Anglo-Saxon Earl, Edwin, in the North Riding around Richmond. And there, on a cliff above the Swale, he began in 1071 to build a magnificent castle which uniquely for these early bastions seems to have been of stone from the outset.

The base of the triangular site and of the great courtyard was the cliff above the Swale. On the other two sides he built massive stone walls with four towers. The principal entrance was through the gatehouse at the apex. The dominating 100ft-high keep, built over the original gatehouse, was added in the 12th century and completed by Henry II. Also added was a second

42 court, called the barbican, outside the gatehouse, a wall enclosing a third court called the cockpit to the east, and the two-storey Scollands Hall which is a very early example of Norman domestic architecture, where the owner had his quarters overlooking the Swale.

The history of the castle is like a roll call of medieval royalty. It was the prison of William the Lion of Scotland taken at Alnwick in 1174. It was frequently in the Crown's ownership. It commands the entrance to Swaledale but has little strategic value. It saw little fighting and was mercifully left unmolested by the Wars of the Roses and the Civil War. King John would have had it destroyed and by 1540 it was recorded as "a mere ruine". But English Heritage still has a castle of first importance in its care.

Two views which show how the castle dominates the town — from the Swale (left) and across a flower meadow

Clifford's Tower, York

We moved from ditches and ramparts to castles, albeit wooden ones, in one epic year in Yorkshire – 1068. And immediately we acquired, directly from William the Conqueror, not one but two castles in York facing each other across the Ouse. In this way he sought to control the river and the Vale of York and dominate the town which had been founded by the Roman 9th Legion in AD71 and subsequently became the Jorvik Viking settlement that gave the current city its name.

One of the castles was on a mound called Baile Hill across Skeldersgate Bridge from the site dominated by Clifford's Tower (right) which in spring stands on a host of dancing daffodils (page 47). We don't know which came first but we do know that one was thrown up in 1069 in eight days after the Northumbrians had caused mayhem.

Not much remains of the Baile Hill castle other than its 40ft-high tree-topped motte (mound) on which the wooden structure stood. It was burned along with the other across the Ouse in 1069 when York rose up in support of the Danish invader. The Norman garrison set fire to houses nearby to deny the revolting populace cover only to see the flames roar out of control throughout the city. The Danes prevailed and demolished both castles.

William hurried North again, rebuilt his castles and promptly embarked on his "Harrying of the North", laying waste to vast tracts of the countryside to cow any who escaped his awesome bloodletting. His coins, along with those of Edward the Confessor, were found in a pot on Old Baile in 1802. Some 160 years earlier the motte was used as a Civil War gun emplacement.

It is quite possible that the more enduring of York's castles was thrown together. Both were

certainly rushed jobs. And the keep known as Clifford's Tower has been remarkably prone to fire – and not merely at the hands of Danes and revolting Yorkshiremen. It was razed to the ground in one awful early example of ethnic cleansing only 15 years after Henry II had received the homage of William, King of the Scots, there in 1175.

The Jewish community had raised hackles by attending Richard the Lionheart's coronation. Their presence was regarded as a bad omen. Persecution followed. In York the Jewish population took refuge in the castle and were besieged when they refused to readmit the sheriff. As violence threatened, fathers slaughtered their entire families and soon the Jews were consumed in a holocaust of fire. Yet another timber castle was built only to be damaged by a great storm in 1225. A quarter of a century later Henry III spent £2,500 on a magnesian limestone castle modelled on the quatrefoil (four overlapping circles) design of that at Etampes.

It has since survived more fire as well as floods and an attempt by a gaoler to sell its stone piecemeal for profit. It was also one of those places that Cromwell knocked about a bit. It was again rebuilt after the Restoration in 1660 with panels over the archway carved with the Royal Arms and those of the Clifford family. Curiously today's ruin still bears the name of an early Lancastrian who was hung in chains from it in 1322.

Bowes

"But Bowes isn't in Yorkshire," I can hear you purists saying. Nor is it. But it used to be when natural boundaries (the Tees) and not Sir Edward Heath's new-fangled political boundaries of 1974 took it into County Durham. And Bowes is part of Yorkshire's Norman fortification. Its castle was erected as a strong watchtower with walls 12ft thick to command the Stainmore pass to Carlisle. It was raised, about 100 years after Richmond, on the site of the former Roman fort, Lavatrae which performed a similar purpose. The fort was used as a quarry for both the castle and the nearby church – a classic example of the recycling of a Roman outpost which was garrisoned by a legion famous for its Spanish horses.

It is thought possible that Alan the Red, builder of Richmond castle, created the first earthworks because Stainmore obviously needed defending against the marauding Scots. But it was left to Henry II, as ward of the heiress of Richmondshire, to raise the castle in 1171. It is a solid, rectangular, sandstone keep which has a moat but none of the usual other fortifications of a Norman castle. Nor was it a comfortable posting. Its function was military, rugged, like the countryside in which it was set, and shorn of domestic comforts, apart from a kitchen on the first floor. They had it better in Roman times. Our Roman conquerors had a bath 27ft long and 18ft wide at the south-east corner of the four-acre site.

Just to emphasise the military nature of Bowes, the Romans had two signal stations a mile apart to the west into the pass. Both are to be found on the north side of the A66. Bowes was thus crucial to Yorkshire's security for at least 1,600 years.

49

Pontefract

Most castles have seen their share of bloodletting but Pontefract, at the heart of what became the Yorkshire coalfield and the liquorice industry, is a very bloody place indeed, as Shakespeare duly recorded. "O Pomfret, Pomfret! O thou bloody prison," he quotes one of its victims, Earl Rivers in *Richard the Third*. The castle was built near the confluence of the Calder and Aire in the first rush of Norman castle construction after 1066 by Ilbert de Lacy, a friend of William's half-brother, the Bishop of Bayeux, whose lands were mainly in the West Riding. Its site is on a rock to the east of what was then known as Tateshalle.

Progressively over the generations the de Lacys created one of the noblest Plantagenet castles in the North and a Royal castle in 1399. The seven-acre site was surrounded by a ditch and wall, defended by five towers and a barbican with a drawbridge. A keep was added in the 13th century and a great gate, flanked by semi-circular towers, in the 14th century. The chief remnant is part of the keep, the battered walls, foundations and dungeons where Roundhead prisoners carved their names.

Henry VIII, Queen Elizabeth I and Charles I enjoyed its hospitality and John of Gaunt entertained Chaucer there. It had something of Windsor about it. Edward IV was there on the eve of his bloody Roses' victory at Towton. But it was also a place where many lost hope. Most infamously of all, Richard II, deprived of his crown and incarcerated there, was murdered within its walls at the behest of Bolingbroke. It was twice besieged by Parliamentarians first in 1645 and then four years later when it was the last place in England to surrender to the Roundheads. It was demolished at the request of garrison-weary Pomfretians.

Sandal

Only eight miles from Pontefract there are the limited remains – fragments of keep and bailey wall, the mound and choked moat – of a local castle at Sandal, Wakefield. It was originally built in wood in the Conqueror's day to the motte and bailey plan by the de Warennes on a hill rising out of the plain through which the Calder flows. Then in the 13th century it was replaced by a stone structure which interestingly was circular like Conisbrough, also associated with the same Warenne family.

The circular outer bailey was surrounded by a ditch and on the motte was a circular barbican connected to a round keep with two attached towers, one semi-circular and the other polygonal. It must have looked very imposing to early Wakefield folk.

It had to wait a long time to enter the history books and curiously its two moments of glory were marked by trickery. First, during the immensely complicated Wars of the Roses, 5,000 Yorkists spent Christmas 1460 there, cheek by jowl with 20,000 Lancastrians at Pontefract. By December 30 the Yorkists had to go foraging for supplies. They encountered a small Lancastrian force. The Duke of York sounded the charge from the castle to rescue them only to be cut to pieces by the waiting main Lancastrian army in the battle of Wakefield Green. Nearly 200 years later the King's commander ordered the drums to beat for prayers and then charged out of the castle to put the besieging Roundheads, also at prayer, to flight. It was a Pyrrhic victory. Parliament ordered Sandal to be made untenable in 1646.

Skipsea

As the sea erodes the Holderness coast, the 45ft-high motte of the old Norman castle at Skipsea may well become an island again. It was on an island in Skipsea Mere that William the Conqueror's Lord of Holderness, Drogo de Brevrere, ingeniously threw up a castle in classic early Norman style in the 1070s. First, he raised the level of the island to form a motte, creating a surrounding ditch with defensive ramparts, and then put a wooden tower on top of it. He reached his castle by a causeway across the mere from an eight-acre kidney-shaped bailey to the west, defended by a ditch and rampart.

Drogo may well have been left to enjoy his fortified island if he had not murdered his wife. This was not necessarily a hanging offence in those days but Drogo's wife was a niece of William the Conqueror. That did for him. His lands were confiscated and allocated, presumably on the basis that lightning never strikes twice, so to speak, to Odo, Count of Champagne, who was married to the Conqueror's sister. Odo did not repeat Drogo's mistake but did rebel against William Rufus (1087-1100) and also forfeited his land.

Henry I bestowed the honour on another treacherous branch of the Norman invaders. To be fair, the second generation, William le Gros was principal commander at the victorious Battle of the Standard in 1138 against the Scots at Northallerton under the sacred banners of four Northern saints. He was otherwise a fully paid up member of the awkward squad and his son abandoned Skipsea in the mid-13th century. The mere was drained in the 18th century, leaving the earthworks high if not dry and now in the care of English Heritage.

Pickering

William the Conqueror raised the first Royal castle at Pickering to control the east-west route along the southern edge of the North York Moors and the north-south York–Malton–Whitby road. For most of its 350-year active life from soon after the Conquest, its role was to provide accommodation for the king and his retinue. Most of the kings between 1100 and 1400 visited it and hunted in the forest which is now a national park. When they were not there it was the sheriff's base. The ruins are remarkably well preserved considering that it was beginning to fall apart by the 1530s.

William's first castle had a circular wooden keep on a motte surrounded by a ditch and fence, with an outer palisade enclosing the inner and outer wards or baileys where the halls and offices were built. Wood was progressively replaced by stone in four phases – 1180-87 on the keep, the Coleman Tower controlling the entrance and the bridge linking the two; then under King John from 1207-10; then under Henry III and finally with the replacement of the wooden outer walls in stone, with three towers and gatehouse, in the early 14th century. The result: a magnificent – indeed, romantic – edifice.

It became the stronghold of the Duke of Lancaster in 1267 when Henry III gave it to his younger son, Edmund Crouchback. His son, Thomas of Lancaster led the barons against his weak cousin Edward II. But Thomas was defeated at Boroughbridge and then executed in Pontefract which, mortifyingly, he also owned. Bolingbroke came to Pickering to claim his inheritance when he landed at the mouth of the Humber from exile to become Henry IV. Since Henry V it has been the responsibility of the Crown and is now an English Heritage attraction.

Tickhill

Roger de Busli was another of William's great Norman nobles who was made for life when he received the Honour of Tickhill with lands in six counties. He chose to defend himself from the Anglo-Saxons – if not all of his estates – on the site of a Brigantian settlement at Tickhill at the southern extremity of Yorkshire only a couple of miles from the Nottinghamshire border. He probably first put a wooden tower inside a palisade on top of a hill called Castle Mount, but between 1080 and 1085 he replaced it with a stone castle there with a moat, gateway tower and drawbridge.

After de Busli's death William Rufus sold the castle at an enormous price to Robert de Belesme who later rebelled against Henry I's move to curb baronial power. He was taken prisoner after a siege and the Crown assumed ownership. Henry II erected a 10-sided shell keep in 1178-79 and he and Queen Eleanor of Aquitaine lived there for a time. His son, Richard the Lionheart, made it one of only five places in England royally licensed to hold jousting tournaments. Tickhill became a place of chivalry.

King John seized it while Richard was away on his crusades but was required by treaty to hand it over along with Nottingham to the King's officers. He refused. Tickhill and Nottingham were besieged and held on even when news of Richard's return home came. When they capitulated, the ringleaders were hanged on Tickhill's walls. It was beseiged again in Edward II's time and then after the Civil War battle of Marston Moor. It was demolished by order of Parliament. Only a gateway tower open to the skies, the moat and a few walls remain. The site is now privately occupied.

Knaresborough

The royal castle which once stood on the cliffs above the Nidd gorge at Knaresborough is now a delightful municipal park and gardens with the backdrop of a ruined keep. Serlo de Burgh, who came over with the Conqueror, founded it about 30 years after the Battle of Hastings. He chose his site well – ravines on three sides and a moat on the other. It was the administrative centre of a 126 square mile royal forest which covered lower Nidderdale. Serlo's nephew, Eustace FitzJohn, made the mistake of joining forces with the Scots and lost his inherited seat of power in 1136.

Knaresborough was rebuilt early in the 14th century when it took on a new lease of life. On his marriage, Edward III settled the town, forest and "new" castle – indeed, the entire Honour of Knaresborough – on his wife, Phillipa. She often spent the summer there and went down in history as the successful pleader for the lives of the burghers at the 1347 siege of Calais. Her records chest is preserved in the guardroom-cum-museum.

There is at least one connection with the other royal castle of Pontefract: Richard II was held at Knaresborough on his way to his murder there.

During the Civil War the Royalist garrison was starved into surrender and in 1646 Parliament ordered the castle which a century earlier Leland found "standith magnificently and strongly on a rock" to be rendered untenable. Today Knaresborough takes its ease amid what the Parliamentarians left and shudders at the hell its prisoners must have experienced in its preserved dungeon.

Middleham

Alan the Red, Lord of Richmond, gave Middleham, commanding the entrance to Wensleydale and Coverdale, to his brother Ribald before 1086. Ribald built a conventional motte and presumably wooden castle, with a bailey, defended by ditches, on William's Hill south west of the village. Then, less than 100 years later, probably his grandson, Robert FitzRanulph, upped sticks and built one of the largest keeps in England in a much less commanding position 500 yards to the north east. This is the wonderful ruin you see today at the centre of arguably Yorkshire's most magnificent castle.

It became a palatial self-contained house and fort but that was only a start. In 1270 it passed by marriage into the hands of the great Yorkist family, the Nevilles who soon replaced the timber palisade with the present magnificent perimeter wall, with towers at each corner. In the early 15th century the fourth Lord Neville then set about making it a principal residence by building chambers and offices inside the perimeter walls. It became an important Yorkist base in the Wars of the Roses and the home of that noble son of York, Richard III. It was here that his son was born to a Neville wife and died 10 years later.

The castle, known as the Windsor of the North, was for centuries a court and military HQ, a magnificent centre of power and influence. A castle become a palace. And then after only two years on the throne Richard fell at Bosworth. And with him died Middleham's glory and grandeur. It was garrisoned during the Civil War and held prisoners. The rest is a long story of decline into a truly magnificent ruin cared for by English Heritage.

Conisbrough

The originator of Conisbrough Castle in industrial south Yorkshire five miles south west of Doncaster was with me in spirit in childhood. I was brought up looking across the Calder Valley to where William de Warenne and his descendants hunted in the Erringden deer forest. But Erringden at Hebden Bridge is 40 miles as the crow flies to the north west, emphasising the extent to which the Normans used Yorkshire for sport, having laid waste to it.

Warenne, the first Earl of Surrey, built his first wooden castle on the site of a Scandinavian king's fortification (Cunugesburh) above the River Don. Within 100 years it passed by marriage to Hameline Plantagenet, a half brother of Henry II. And Hameline proceeded to replace it with a circular keep, with six mighty buttresses, in local magnesian limestone which even in ruin had Nikolaus Pevsner raving about it – "in the beauty of its geometrical simplicity and of its large ashlar facing unsurpassed in England". It is also the oldest circular keep in England – an important design development against mining and sapping which Hameline used in another castle in Normandy.

The ruins – the 90ft-tall keep, massive buttresses, barbican, inner bailey and walls also deeply impressed Sir Walter Scott when he first saw it from a mail coach in 1801. It became his setting for *Ivanhoe*. Its stone has remained astonishingly clean for a castle which came for more than a century to look beautifully incongruous amid coal mining and heavy industry. Visitors can see various rooms and chambers and their huge fireplaces.

Scarborough

The 300ft-high cliffs forming a headland reached across a narrow neck of land and dividing Scarborough's north and south bays were made for a fortress. Bronze Age man recognised this 2,500 years ago. The Romans used it as a look-out station and the Vikings settled below the cliff, lending their name to the town – Skarthi's stronghold. It would have been astonishing if the Normans, in their urge to control their new domain, had not built a castle there. And, of course, they did, but not legitimately. You were supposed to get the King's permission. Otherwise your "adulterine" castle might be demolished or forfeited. William le Gros, the awkward squad who built Skipsea Castle, fortified Castle Hill in a spate of private enterprise. He also got away with it during the anarchy of King Stephen's reign until Henry II set about curbing the power of the barons and grabbed it for himself.

Within four years of being crowned in 1154 he started building his first and most powerful castle which became the royal fortress visitors to the Spa see crowning the headland today. It was never taken by force – only by trickery or starvation. Plantagenet kings – and notably King John and Henry III – spent fortunes on maintaining the stronghold. It was in decay by the end of the 14th century but it defied Parliament and its gunpowder on two occasions during the Civil War and so eventually earned

The still mightily impressive remains of Henry II's most powerful fortress at Scarborough from the North Bay

itself a Parliamentary demolition order.

But you can't keep a good castle down. It was then used as a barracks and a prison and garrisoned during the Jacobite rebellion and the threat of Napoleonic invasion. It was in use as a barracks until the German cruisers, *Derfflinger* and *Von der Tann* shelled it in 1914. English Heritage now cares for it.

The remains of the castle keep (left) and a view across Scarborough's South Bay

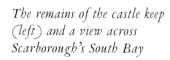

Helmsley

The spectacular castle in the lovely town of Helmsley, backing on to the North York Moors, was in the second wave of Norman fortifications. It might have been in the first had Robert de Mortain, a half brother of William the Conqueror, done his duty. William Rufus confiscated his estates in 1088 and we know nothing more until 1120 when Walter Espec, described as "a valiant soldier of the Conqueror", emerges as a strengthener of the kingdom's defences against the Scots. He built the first Helmsley castle in wood on a rock at the centre of his estates inside a great ringwork. He also founded Kirkham and Reivaulx abbeys. He has thus left magnificent marks on North Yorkshire.

He died without heir in 1154 and his estates passed through marriage to the de Roos family. The castle substantially remained with them until 1688. Robert de Roos, also known as Fursan as Helmsley Castle is sometimes called, rebuilt it in limestone and sandstone after 1186 – no keep, but twin towers, a stone curtain wall with round towers at each corner and two entrances, north and south, with towers. The castle was remodelled by later generations and a great hall was added as castles generally began to be converted for peaceful living. A Tudor mansion was also built within the west of the twin towers.

Eventually Helmsley came into the possession of that rake, libertine and thoroughly bad lot, George Villiers, the first Duke of Buckingham, who, not surprisingly, did nothing to improve it. Nor did the Civil War. Having escaped action throughout the Middle Ages, Helmsley was beseiged by Parliament in 1644. The Royalists were starved out and the Roundheads rendered the fortress unusable. English Heritage now looks after the ruins.

Skipton

You have to thank a very exceptional woman for one of the best preserved castles in England which stands proudly, its gate flanked by fat semi-circular walls, at the top of Skipton's main street welcoming visitors. She was Lady Anne Clifford, the last of the bellicose Lancastrian Cliffords. Her castle was starved into submission by the Roundheads in 1645 and then rendered incapable of use in war. But the formidable Lady Anne persuaded Parliament to allow her to restore it, provided the roofs were not capable of mounting cannon. The castle you can explore today is substantially the one she left.

Its story begins when William the Conqueror granted lands in the Dales to Robert de Romille. For his wooden castle, he chose a rock which falls to the north into Eller Beck and a bailey sloping down to the top of the present High Street to guard the gateway to the Dales. That didn't last long. Nor did the Romilles. The Honour of Skipton was subsequently held by the Albemarles, the Crown and even Piers Gaveston, Edward II's obsession, until the barons captured him in Scarborough Castle and beheaded him without trial. Edward II then bestowed it on the Cliffords around 1312.

The family lost it when "Butcher" Clifford fell on the eve of Towton. His son, Henry, was condemned to death but was hidden away in Yorkshire and brought up as a shepherd. No sooner had Henry VII established the House of Tudor after Bosworth than the illiterate shepherd turned up in the Lords to claim his rightful inheritance. His grandson, George, was a great navigator at the time of the Armada and singed the beard of the King of Spain a lot in the West Indies. His collection of seashells is reputed to decorate a room in the castle.

On the right is the castle's entrance gateway. The tiny room below leads to the dungeon

Ravensworth

Yorkshire's castles clearly impressed Sir Walter Scott. Ravensworth, near Richmond, features in his poem *Rokeby*, just as Conisbrough was the setting for his novel, *Ivanhoe*. It stands between Swaledale and Teesdale, south of the A66 and Stanwick's Brigantian fortifications, remote and bleak on the edge of the village close to the border with County Durham. The Anglo-Saxon Lords of Ravensworth have left nothing tangible of their presence in these Pennine foothills. The ruins take us back to the Norman Fitz-Hughs who flourished in these wild parts from Henry II to Henry VII (1180-1500).

Today's remaining fragments, mounds, 14th-century gatehouse and adjoining archway, high enough to take a man on horseback and with a portcullis groove, show that the castle was extensive. The tower had 17ft-square rooms inside 5ft-thick walls with fireplaces and narrow windows. It must have been bracing to live there. One of the Fitz-Hughs, Henry went to war with Henry V with 66 men-at-arms and 209 archers. He also fought against the Turks, made a pilgrimage to Jerusalem and visited Cairo. He returned to be buried in Jervaulx Abbey. Not much seems to have disturbed the even tenor of Ravensworth's ways over the centuries.

The Fitz-Hughs poured money into the castle in the 14th century. A hundred years on, Leland, in his very frank itinerary of castles, gave not a hint of decay, even if he wasn't impressed: "Excepting 2 or 3 square towers...nothing memorable in it". It was then owned by Lord Parr. It was held by the Crown from 1571-1629 and then by a succession of private owners. The ruins in sheep pasture have not changed a lot in 150 years.

Hazelwood Castle

You can live very well indeed in Hazelwood Castle which was owned continuously by the Vavasours for well over 800 years. For the last four years it has been a high class hotel in a park just off the Leeds-York A64 road near Tadcaster. It overlooks the Vale of Towton whose Cod Beck ran red with blood at the murderous Roses' battle in a snowstorm in 1461.

The Vavasours, a distinguished sounding lot, had humble beginnings. Indeed, their very name means they received land from nobles not the king. But they persevered in Norman times and in 1286 were granted the building of a chapel, the only remaining part of the castle complete in medieval form. Four years later they were given a licence to crenellate. Sir William Vavasour quarried the lovely magnesian limestone for the castle from his estate and supplied it for the construction of York Minister. Another Vavasour was knighted at Flodden Field and Sir Thomas equipped ships and men to sail against the Armada. In return, Elizabeth I turned a blind eye to his Roman Catholicism and his family enjoyed unwonted freedom of worship in their chapel. When the family sold the castle in 1908 provision was made for continued RC worship. The chapel is a store of Vavasour monuments. The main building is attributed to Sir Walter le Vavasour in the 18th century.

Over the past century the castle has been successively a private residence, a maternity home and a Carmelite friary until it became a hotel. No doubt the good Vavasours would approve of its conversion to good living.

Whorlton

The origins of Whorlton Castle on the northern slope of the once iron-rich Cleveland Hills are lost in time. It is supposed that the original motte and bailey castle, surrounded by a 60ft-wide ditch, was a wooden construction perhaps by Robert, Earl of Mortain, during the first part of the 12th century. He held "Wirveltune", as the Domesday scribes named the place.

Nikolaus Pevsner described Whorlton-in-Cleveland as "an eerie place, with a castle in ruins, a church in ruins and hardly anything else". He was a bit hard on the castle. The magnificent oblong gatehouse tower and plain tunnel-vaulted cellars we can see today, with the remains of a medieval garden, ponds and park to the east, probably came about 200 years after the original castle during Richard II's reign (1377-99) They were the work of the de Meynells who held it until the manor passed by marriage in the mid 14th century to the Darcys and then, a century later, to the Strangewayes. It eventually came into the hands of the Crown during Henry VIII's time and remained in royal hands for a good 100 years until it passed to the Scottish Bruces. Above the gateway are three shields bearing the arms of Darcy, Meynell and Grey. The Crown didn't look after it and by 1600 it was described as "old and ruinous".

Among those who lived here was the Earl of Lennox whose son, Darnley, married Mary Queen of Scots. Tradition has it that Whorlton saw the intrigues which led to that ill-fated marriage. Altogether, Whorlton has had its fill of tragedy. The plague reduced its population to 10 and the remains of the medieval village are nearby.

Kilton

The bastion of the de Brus, and through marriage of the Thwengs and Lumleys, is not the easiest of Yorkshire's northern defensive line of castles to find. It is called Kilton and lies buried in private woods on a knoll above the Kilton Beck, just over a mile south west of Loftus, the old iron and steel town in the North York Moors. It seems to have been by-passed by the stirring events of Yorkshire's history. Perhaps this is tribute to its impregnable site which is reflected in its name and that of the main family which held it, the Thwengs.

Kilton derives from the old English for a "farmstead near the club-shaped hill" and Thweng (or Thwing) is Old Scandinavian for "a narrow strip of land". Precisely. That is what the remains of Kilton stand on. It is a rather elongated castle, narrow north to south and long from its western entrance to the eastern cliff over the beck where the ruins – of a tower – stand highest. There is a piece of Norman curtain wall moving west and the remains of a couple of towers. The castle entrance to the west was protected by a deep ditch. Records show that it was one of the castles on which major construction work took place in the 14th century.

This could mean that the de Brus originally had a wooden castle here in William Rufus' reign, that it was strengthened by the Thwengs and that a Lumley – Sir Marmaduke, son of a Thweng mother – created the formidable fortress we can imagine today. This is because the last of the Thwengs, a priest, died about the middle of the 14th century.

Harewood

Peeping out of the Harewood estate as you climb Harewood Bank on the A61 are the remains of Harewood Castle built into the hillside above the Wharfe like so many later and much more modest properties in the old West Riding. The oblong structure, rising 90ft like a tower block and with walls 7ft thick, is in private ownership. It is regarded as the most important example in Yorkshire of a medieval castle built as a single bastion without courtyard, baileys or curtain walls. It was the work of Sir William Aldburgh who secured a licence to crenellate in 1367.

The entrance, high enough to admit a man on horseback, bears the Aldburgh's fatalistic motto: "What shall be, shall". It has a portcullis groove and two shields, one of the Aldburghs and the other of the Baliols because, some say, the banished King of Scotland was given refuge here. Because of the lie of the land, the great hall occupies the ground instead of more usually the first floor.

The most interesting thing about Harewood's history is the number of families which have owned it – the Redmans and Rythers, through Aldburgh's daughters, until Elizabethan times, then the Gascoignes, the Wentworths, the Cutlers and the Boulters until Henry Lascelles, ancestor of the Earl of Harewood, acquired the estate in 1721. His son started to build the magnificent house and grounds in 1759.

Bolton Castle

As early as 1379, Yorkshire's castles were undergoing a subtle change. While still looking militarily impressive, they were making concessions to domestic comfort and even aesthetics. Bolton Castle, dominating Wensleydale, and now a tourist showpiece, reflects the changing balance. It is, indeed, described as the climax of English military architecture and its formidable four-square, four-corner-tower design with ranges enclosing a courtyard was immediately and closely followed by Sheriff Hutton, Wressle and Danby.

It was built by Richard Scrope, Richard II's Lord Chancellor, and its remarkably well-preserved remains with walls up to 9ft thick are still occupied by his direct descendants. He spent the then immense sum of £12,000 on it over 18 years. Its stone was quarried nearby and the timber brought from Cumberland. Perhaps it was because of its relative comfort that Queen Elizabeth I chose it to incarcerate Mary Queen of Scots there in 1568 until she briefly escaped. Her custodian, Sir Francis Knollys, wrote that year "It appeareth to be very strong, very fair and very stately after the old manner of building…It is the highest walled house that I have seen." Note his use of the word house.

For all its impression of strength, it had no protective moat or ditch or drawbridge and was eventually surrounded by landscaped grounds and walled deer parks. Yet it held out against a Parliamentarian siege for more than a year in 1644-45. Its north-west tower was weakened by bombardment and Parliament ordered the castle to be made untenable. It still looks tremendous.

Sheriff Hutton

It seems scarcely credible today but from the ruins now forming a farmyard of the once magnificent castle at Sheriff Hutton, 10 miles north of York, emerged the queen of the first Tudor king. It was also the home of one of Yorkshire's great families, the Nevilles. The story starts around 1140 with the second wave of Norman castle building. Bertram de Bulmer ran up a castle on another site which can be seen near today's church. This first Sheriff Hutton castle marked, the experts tell us, a transition from motte and bailey to keep and bailey. When he became Sheriff of Yorkshire, Bulmer prefixed Sheriff to the name of the village.

The castle eventually passed by marriage to the Nevilles who obtained a licence to crenellate in 1381. They erected almost a carbon copy of Bolton Castle, licensed two years earlier, and today's ruins give you some idea of its original magnificence. They lost it when Richard Neville, Earl of Warwick, known as the Kingmaker, was killed in the Roses battle of Barnet in 1471.

Edward IV then granted it to his brother, that noble son of York, Richard of Gloucester, who counted Sheriff Hutton with Middleham as his favourite homes both before and after he briefly became Richard III. It was at Sheriff Hutton that he imprisoned his niece, Elizabeth of York, sister of the two little princes murdered in the Tower. He had designs on marrying her until he perished on Bosworth field. Then Henry Tudor (Henry VII) summoned her to London to make her his queen and give her a son, Henry VIII. By then the castle's days of glory were nearly over. It was still "princely" in 1535 but by 1618 it was decaying. *Sic transit gloria.*

Wressle

Nikolaus Pevsner sweepingly described Wressle as "the only castle fragment of any importance in the East Riding". Only the shell of the south range and remains of the Lord's and Chapel Towers still stand of the original. It is with Bolton and Sheriff Hutton, one of the family of castles, all erected around 1380. Leland, the chronicler of castles, saw it in its complete state in the 16th century and said it had five towers, one at each corner and another over the gatehouse in the middle of the east range. It was, he said, one of the most "proper" north of the Trent.

It lies beside the Leeds-Hull railway line between Selby and Howden on the banks of the River Derwent. It was built for Sir Thomas Percy and passed into the hands of the main Earls of Northumberland branch of the family in the 15th century. While fortified and defensive, it was,

like Bolton and Sheriff Hutton, moving from military establishment to grand mansion. This was noted by Leland around 1540. He reported "the hall and the great chambers be fair, and so is the chapel and the closets. One thing I liked exceedingly in one of the towers, that was a study called Paradise". He also mentioned the "exceedingly fair" gardens within the moat and the orchards outside.

There is no doubt that under the Northumberlands Wressle became a lavish place indeed. But it did not survive the Civil War. The Earl, a Parliamentarian himself, was shabbily rewarded. The Roundhead garrison vandalised his castle and estate and Parliament, after a lot of tooing and froing, ordered him in 1650 to demolish his very own ancient pile to prevent it being used again. They did it for him while he was pleading for it to be spared.

Ripley

Legend has it that the first Ingilby to settle in 1320 at Ripley, above the River Nidd, four miles north of Harrogate, saved Edward III when he was attacked by a wild boar while hunting in Knaresborough Forest. The king rewarded Sir Thomas de Ingilby, as he was called, by giving him freedom to hunt in the forest and in 1357 a charter for an annual market and horsefair.

The Ingilbys have been here ever since and the 29th of the line, another Sir Thomas, occupies what is truly a home – and a rich museum of a home – as well as a castle. It is open to the public and set in a beautiful "Capability" Brown deer park with a lake and a walled garden and next to a model village which was rebuilt in the 1830s by Sir William Amcotts Ingilby in Alsace-Lorraine style.

The gatehouse, built to keep out the Scots, opens on to a courtyard and dates from 1450.

The tower block of the original castle also remains. Otherwise, it was made largely new in 1780. The relics on show recall a history packed with 17th-century incident. James I was an overnight guest in the Tower Room in 1603. The Ingilbys, staunch Roman Catholics, were implicated in the Guy Fawkes plot to blow up Parliament. Forty years later "Trooper" Jane Ingilby rode off to fight for the king at Marston Moor. She returned home wounded but still gave Cromwell an uncomfortable night in the castle library, keeping her loaded pistol unwaveringly on the unwelcome victor as he rested. She probably regretted she didn't shoot him. Hollows in the east wall of the church are said to have been made by Cromwell's troopers when they shot and missed in executing Ripley men taken prisoner.

Danby

To look at it now, you would not think that Danby Castle was once as grand as Bolton, Sheriff Hutton and Wressle castles. Its plan is essentially theirs, except that its corner towers instead of standing four square project diagonally outwards. The remains on the tip of Danby Rigg, are now incorporated in a privately-owned farm a mile south east of the village which lies deep in the North York Moors National Park in the upper reaches of the Esk Valley.

John de Nevill received a licence to crenellate in 1382 – exactly the same period as Bolton, Sheriff Hutton and Wressle – and created a magnificent if compact quadrangular palace fortress with the five storey towers linked with ranges of similar height. The inner courtyard is a mere 50 by 22.5ft. There are no traceable moat, ditches or earthworks. But the chronicler Leland, visiting Danby in 1534, "saw no house in the north so like a princely loggings". Catherine Parr, the last of Henry VIII's six wives, lived here for a time.

The ranges and much of the towers may have gone but the original doorway leads to the throne room where the Danby Court Leet and Baron meets once a year, as it has done from Elizabethan times. It administers common land and rights of way over the 11,000-acre Danby estate and, among other things, the gathering of sphagnum moss which used to be used in stuffing mattresses but now for flower arranging. This castle by the roadside leads a very workaday existence which seems to have been its fate in life.

Snape

Snape, like Danby, is a Neville castle – they seem to have acquired an "e" at the end of their name along life's road – and is distinguished as the house which Catherine Parr left in 1543 to become Henry VIII's sixth and last wife and, clever girl, ultimately his widow. It lies three miles west of the Great North Road (A1) and a similar distance south of Bedale in a lovely sylvan setting.

Catherine Parr lived here as the wife of John Neville, Lord Latimer, her second marriage. When he died, she somehow came to the notice of the king and is reputed to have said, with much Yorkshire common sense, that in view of his history it would be better to be his mistress than his wife. She turned out to be a wife of courage, dignity and erudition. And when Henry VIII died, she married Sir Thomas Seymour, brother of Jane Seymour, to whom she had been intended before King Henry stepped in to claim her.

The chapel where she worshipped is still there and in use amid the ruins. The earliest castle was built by the FitzRanulphs, of Middleham, in the 12th century and was succeeded by a Neville castle built around 1425 on the quadrangular lines of Bolton. A later form to a similar design is reputed to be the work of the second Lord Burghley. It was "a goodly castel", according to Leland, the chronicler, when Catherine left it to become Queen.

Cawood

Two of Yorkshire's castles – Cawood and Crayke – have close associations with the church. Cawood, on the banks of the Ouse, just downstream from its confluence with the Wharfe, four miles north west of Selby, was the palace of the Archbishops of York from the 12th century. As such, it was not only the residence of the leading political figures of medieval England but also the economic and administrative centre of their estate.

But Cawood's story begins long before then. King Edgar granted a vast estate to the archbishop in 963. A licence to crenellate was issued in 1271 to Archbishop Gifford. In 1465 George Neville, brother of Warwick the Kingmaker, celebrated his appointment to the archbishopric with one of the biggest banquets ever held in England – 2,000 cooks using 100 oxen, 500 deer and 1,000 sheep. Not surprisingly, if this is how they lived, seven archbishops died there.

Their castle-palace was frequented by kings and queens from Edward I who held some of his Parliaments there. Henry VIII and Elizabeth I passed through its gates. Cardinal Wolsey came to reside at Cawood and employed 300 workmen on its repair. He was arrested for high treason here in his bedchamber by the Earl of Northumberland on that fateful day for Tudor England – November 4, 1530. Queen Mary's soldiers deposed the Protestant Archbishop Holgate and ransacked the castle. And the Royalist garrison was ousted in the Civil War. Parliament had no doubt it was a castle rather than a palace. It ordered it to be made untenable in 1647.

The remains of Cawood Castle remind us of its glitteringly golden past. They date from the 15th century — a three-storey stone gatehouse, an adjacent two-storey hall in brick and stone and the castle garth enclosure which had a garden, fishponds and a claypit

Crayke

They have fortified the hill top at Crayke, a couple of miles north east of Easingwold, for at least 1,400 years. Legend has it that it was a redoubt long before Egfrith, King of Northumberland, gave Crayke to St Cuthbert, of Durham, in 685 as a resting place between Lindisfarne and York. St Cuthbert's monastery there was subsequently put to the torch by the Danish invaders. One of the Norman bishops of Durham, reputedly Hugh Pudsay, erected a motte and bailey castle adjacent to the existing structure. This was replaced around 1450 "totally by Neville, Bishop of Durdome (Durham)" according to Leland, writing in Henry VIII's time.

In fact, it seems Neville put up two separate buildings. The privately owned one we see today is the Great Chamber, a commanding four-storey tower house with a castellated rear wing built above the surviving vaulted undercroft of a medieval kitchen. The other, the adjacent so-called "New Tower", is in ruins.

Given its long ecclesiastical connection with Durham, Crayke might, for all its battlements, be more reasonably regarded as a fortified house. But again the Parliamentarians did not see it like that. They ordered it to be made untenable in 1647 and it was partly demolished in 1650. There is an hilarious side to Crayke. As the gift of a king, it was for centuries – indeed, until the Reform Act of 1832 – in the County of Durham, even though it is 25 miles inside Yorkshire. This led to all sorts of jumping in and out of Crayke by debtors dodging Yorkshire and Durham writs.

Spofforth

Although Spofforth, halfway between Wetherby and Harrogate, has had a "castle" for at least 800 years, the rather splendid ruins in pinky-brown sandstone are generally regarded as those of a fortified house. It was one of the great Percy family's five properties in Yorkshire. They used it to manage their estates rather than live there. It is remarkable for how many times they lost it and won it back.

The Percys came over with the Conqueror and built a timber manor house near where the present castle stands. Henry de Percy put up the first castle in 1309 but it was confiscated almost 100 years later when another Henry rebelled against Henry IV and was slain at the battle of Bramham Moor. The family got it back after it had been conferred for life on Sir Thomas Rokeby, then Sheriff of Yorkshire. In 1461, the Yorkists laid waste to the mansion and estate after killing another Henry Percy, Earl of Northumberland and his brother at Towton. Then in 1559, yet another Henry was granted a licence to fortify Spofforth. The Percys occupied it for about 50 years before handing it over to their steward around 1600. The end came 50 years later when the victorious Parliamentarians wrecked it during the Civil War.

This demonstrates how the house – described as "extensive and extremely interesting" by Nikolaus Pevsner – evolved over time. It was built in the form of a parallelogram 135ft from north to south and 50ft east to west and made clever use of the fall of the land to the west. To the east, it backs into the rock so that a doorway leads straight into the first floor containing, typically for castles, the great hall. The north-west corner has a polygonal stair turret with a spire.

West Ayton

Just off the Pickering-Scarborough road where the Derwent emerges from Forge Valley the remains of Ayton Castle stand on rising ground above the stream. It was initially the site of a medieval manorial centre, with a hall, ranges of service buildings and a curtain wall with a gatehouse. Some of these were demolished in the late 14th century when the rectangular, three-storey stone tower we can see today was erected by Sir Ralph Eure.

This pele tower or tower house was built in the style more characteristic of Northumberland, of which Sir Ralph was a native, and the Scottish Borders. It is claimed it was a defence against Scottish raiders but there is no evidence that it was ever attacked. It was, in fact, built more for living than defensive purposes. The last recorded occupant died in 1679 and the property has slowly gone to ruin. The vaulted basement is intact but no other floors survive.

But the site has the hallmarks of a high status medieval centre. The tower and the remains of the earlier hall stand within an almost square enclosure 110 by 100yds. Cut into the hillside above are three terraces for gardens or agriculture and below is a line of fishponds running parallel with the river. Ayton may have been decaying for 350 years but it once had a sense of importance.

Hutton Colswain Hall

The mounds on a steep slope overlooking the Derwent in Low Hutton (which with High Hutton forms Huttons Ambo) three miles south west of Malton are thought to be a monument to Norman class-consciousness. It may also be the origin of "ringworks" – an earthwork enclosing a hall of wood or stone which have been found in other parts of England and Wales. The site is called Hutton Colswain Hall, circa 13th century. And thereby hangs a tale.

Colswain, who gave his name to the manor of Hutton Colswain, was presumably a naturalised Scandinanvian. He held the manor by virtue of the "sergeanty" of keeping the gate of the king's castle at York. But a sergeant was far too low in the pecking order to have a full blown castle with motte. So, he had the next best thing: an earthwork enclosure, measuring 32 by 50yds internally, protected by a bank. It was entered at the north-eastern corner through what is thought to have been a gatetower.

Those who excavated the site in 1953 found there had been two succcessive, crudely-built halls – one in wood, 12 by 6.5yds, with entries at each gable end, and a stone building, 16 by 9yds, with an aisle down one side in Scandianvian style. There may also have been a sort of stone tower in the south-west corner, its base having been laid directly on the ground. You've got to admire Sgt. Colswain. If he couldn't have a castle, he was darned well going to have a fortified hall. And he did.

Slingsby

Six miles on the road from Malton to Helmsley, Ryedale boasts a "castle" which was never completed and never a home. But Slingsby Castle – in reality a magnificent fortified Elizabethan house – makes a splendid ruin with corner turrets, high walls, mullioned windows, vaulted cellars and a tremendous moat.

It started life back in the Conqueror's day and is one of the several fortifications erected across Yorkshire by the de Mowbrays which have all but disappeared. Roger de Mowbray is supposed to have built a castle here in the forest on land given to him by William I. It was probably only a lodge. His family kept it until 1322 when John de Mowbray, rebelling against Edward II, was executed after the battle of Boroughbridge. One Ralph de Hastings then acquired Slingsby and in 1338 secured a licence to convert the Mowbray's home into a castle and park. The Mowbrays got their property back, courtesy of Edward III, but it is not clear whether it was them or Hastings who dug the moat 30ft deep and 90ft wide. It is not clear whether it was wet or dry but, either way, it was a formidable barrier.

The impressive house whose ruins we can now see was built around 1620 by Sir Charles Cavendish, dwarf, courageous soldier, philosopher, mathematician and "a lovely and beautiful soul". But the poor chap fought on the losing Royalist side at Marston Moor and had to run for his life. After passing through the hands of the Dukes of Newcastle and Buckingham and the Earl of Carlisle, it became, among other things, a quarry for cottages in the village. But splendid it remains as part of the Castle Howard estate.

Hornby

Four miles north west of Bedale in North
Yorkshire are the remains of a pile which was
home down the centuries to the St Quintins, the
Conyers, the Darcys, the Earls of Holdernesse (as
the Darcys became) and finally, until 1930, to the
Duke of Leeds. It was built by the St Quentins in
the 14th century and grew around a courtyard. Of
the castle itself only one of the four ranges – the
south range – and the so-called keep to the rear
remain. The other ranges were felled 70 years ago.

According to Leland, the chronicler of castles in
Henry VIII's day, Hornby, "the chiefest house of
Lord Conyers" was "but a meane thing" before
the first of that line set about making something
of it around 1500. The main rebuilding was done
by the Holdernesses in the 18th century.

Hornby is thus the story of so many castles
which escaped war and retribution – their
progressive conversion to gracious living.

Gilling

Five miles west of Slingsby, lying strategically between the Hambledon and Howardian Hills, you come to Gilling Castle, standing impressively on Moat Hill above Gilling East village. It is the preparatory school for Ampleforth College. Occupying three sides of a spacious courtyard, the east is an Elizabethan house and the west an 18th-century mansion. Both were the work of the Fairfax family who were connected with Gilling for 406 years.

The main block is much older and within it is part of the original 14th-century castle erected by Thomas de Etton in the style of a Northumbrian pele tower as a defence against hit-and-run Scots. At 80ft square, it is claimed to be the largest tower house in England, with 8ft-thick walls. The Fairfaxes came to possess it by petition in 1489 – 150 years after the marriage of Elizabeth de Etton to a Fairfax.

Three Fairfaxes played a notable role in the development of Gilling. The first did so simply by surviving. Sir Nicholas Fairfax became one of the wonders of his day as a Roman Catholic for opposing and surviving Henry VIII's reforms. Miraculously Gilling remained in Fairfax hands for Nicholas's son, William, to modernise the Etton tower house and introduce a magnificent wood-panelled great chamber, its walls and stained glass windows ablaze with Yorkshire and Fairfax heraldry. Then in the early 18th century Viscount William Emley – as Fairfaxes became known by buying a Tipperary title – brought Tudor Gilling into the Georgian age. It now educates boys for the second Elizabethan.

Burton Agnes Old Hall

There are two halls at Burton Agnes half way between Bridlington and Driffield. One is Jacobean and the other – which interests me – is a medieval jewel cared for by English Heritage. It isn't usually regarded as a fortified house and it isn't castellated. But it is built on classic fortified style – the arched entrance leading into an impressive vaulted stone undercroft with the main hall on the first floor

What is more its three floors were built around 1170-80, probably by Roger de Stuteville, immediately before Richard the Lionheart came to the throne. Like me, you may find it amazing that any Norman family would put up a substantial property in those disturbed days without thought for their personal protection, given what they had done a century earlier to Yorkshiremen in their harrying of the North. I shall be interested to see how the purists argue their way out of this impeccable Yorkshire logic.

The building we see today dates from many periods but there is original 12th century stonework in the west and north walls. At the rear there is a large 12th-century well with a 17th-century donkey wheel for drawing up the water.

Markenfield Hall

Hidden down a farm track to Hellwath just off the A61 road to Harrogate three miles south of Ripon is the finest example of a medieval moated farmhouse in the North. It is Markenfield Hall, a working farm and the home of the 7th Lord Grantley. It goes back to 1310. That was when Exchequer Chancellor John de Markenfield was given a licence to crenellate. His descendants lost the property when they joined in the Catholic Rising of the North in 1569 in support of Mary Queen of Scots. Elizabeth I confiscated it and handed it over to the Lord Keeper, Sir Thomas Egerton.

The new owner built the Tudor gatehouse which is approached on the south side across a bridge over the moat. This water defence encloses a quadrangle with ranges to the north, east and west. The main range is opposite the gatehouse, the main house in the north-east corner and the farm house is on the eastern side.

In the late 18th century, Fletcher Norton, Speaker of the House of Commons and Baron Grantley of Markenfield from 1782, bought the property. He subsequently moved four miles to Grantley Hall but his descendants preserve Markenfield in its working glory.

Nappa Hall

Deep in Metcalfe country just over a mile east of Askrigg, high in Wensleydale, is one of the few surviving medieval fortified houses in the Yorkshire Dales. It is Nappa Hall, a privately occupied fortified manor house which was built in 1459 by Thomas Metcalfe who fought at Agincourt. It is a south facing single-storey hall with a four-storey tower and turret at one end and a lower two-storey block at the other housing the kitchen and service rooms. Both towers have crenellated parapets.

It is a fine example of a fortified dwelling built to protect a family of some importance from Scottish raiders. The Metcalfes were classed as minor gentry but they were of great significance in Wensleydale, serving as estate stewards for the abbots of Jervaulx and the king's wardens in the Forest of Wensleydale. They grew in power and at the end of the Middle Ages were said to be the largest family in England. They were certainly not known for any difficulty in producing male heirs.

Nor were they above flaunting their power. Sir Christopher Metcalfe, High Sheriff of Yorkshire, met the judges of assize at York at the head of 300 Metcalfes all mounted on white horses. They lived at Nappa until 1756. Mary Queen of Scots stayed there during her imprisonment and her ghost is said to haunt the hall.

Marmion Tower

The powerful Marmion family had a castle by the River Ure at West Tanfield on the road from Ripon to Masham from about the time of the Magna Carta. The only surviving bit of it is a fortified gatehouse known as the Marmion Tower which is now a small house of distinction. It is embattled with a stair turret and has a lovely oriel window on the first floor. The gatehouse arch did not have a portcullis but great wooden doors and there is a built-in porter's lodge.

The tower was built of ashlar sandstone by Sir Henry Fitzhugh around 1410. He married a Marmion heiress and their son became Bishop of London. The early 13th-century church of St Nicholas was built astonishingly close to the castle and gatehouse and contains many effigies of the Marmions who were clearly devoted to this lovely spot. It is now open to the public and cared for by English Heritage.

Barden Tower

One of the marks left by the Cliffords of Skipton Castle on the old West Riding is a ruined tower house on the edge of the moors looking up to Simon's Seat above a beautiful stretch of Wharfedale, north of Bolton Abbey. It is Barden Tower which is said to have been a Clifford hunting lodge. All one can say is that the Cliffords built their lodges big and strong – this ran to three storeys – and no doubt as a refuge against Scots marauders.

The tower was rebuilt around 1485 by one of Yorkshire's more romantic souls, Henry Clifford, the so-called Shepherd Lord. He was the son of "Butcher" Clifford who died fighting for the Lancastrian cause, leaving two sons. They were hidden away lest they be put to the Yorkist sword. But when, 15 years later, Henry VII, our first Tudor monarch, brought about a reconciliation by marrying Elizabeth of York from Sheriff Hutton, people began to emerge from the woodwork or, in the case of Henry Clifford, from the hills. This horny handed, illiterate son of toil, as he had perforce become, was proclaimed the heir by his mother. He walked the floor of the House of Lords to claim his castle at Skipton and later re-built Barden Tower.

The tower was restored after the Civil War by Lady Anne Clifford who also built a chapel attached to a cottage at the side. The Shepherd Lord and the now roofless ruins of his tower inspired Wordsworth in writing *The White Doe of Rylstone*.

Mortham Tower

Right on the old Yorkshire–Durham border formed by the Tees, where the Greta joins it, stand the ruins of another fortification which had Sir Walter Scott in raptures in his poem *Rokeby*. It is Mortham Tower just east of Rokeby Hall where Scott was guest of his friend, John Bacon Morritt. It has tourelles – towers corbelled to stand out from the wall – and upright window openings for battlements. The tower itself stands at the corner of a courtyard with a low curtain wall, battlements and a wall walk.

The Rokebys held the manor from the Conqueror right through the Civil War when they were forced to sell. Their original castle is recorded as having been burned down by the Scots in 1314. They then erected Mortham Tower which was again rebuilt in the style of a Borders pele tower in the 15th century when new living quarters were added, including a magnificently beamed great hall. The three rooks of the Rokeby arms are on its wall. Rokeby Hall, on the site of the original castle, was built by Sir Thomas Robinson whose family bought the estate from the Rokebys.

Paull Holme Tower

We move in one great sweep from Mortham's Northern extremity of Yorkshire to its very southern boundary on the Humber – to the village of Paull downstream of Hull where male villagers were required to row the Lord and Lady of the Manor across the river to Lindsey. Here there is a three-storey late medieval tower, probably built at the end of the 15th century at the north end of an existing timber-framed manor house. It was for defensive purposes and, not surprisingly, is more like Lincolnshire brick towers – it is, in fact, built in alternate courses of red and dark blue bricks – than the pele towers of the Border country in the north. It has a brick-vaulted basement.

Paull Holme Tower was originally the home of the Holme family who took their name from the place rather than bestowing theirs on it. The 30ft-high tower is the only bit of the Holmes' fortified house which remains. An adjacent farm was built out of the hall's materials in 1837. The tower shrinks or tapers a little floor by floor but the parapet projects slightly, with a rather pleasing effect for a fortification.

Paull village has done many things in its time – commercial fishing, especially for shrimps and eels, shipbuilding, and providing a battery to defend the Humber from Henry VIII's time until World War II and the site of a lighthouse during the 19th century. Its medieval tower is now reputed to be haunted by a cow which somehow climbed the staircase to the battlements but could not get back down and jumped to its death over the top.

York's Walls

Let it not be said this book cannot see the wood for the trees. After all, they didn't enclose a city with walls for the hell of it but to keep hell out. What is more, York's walls are the longest and best maintained in England – some two miles long. Its gates and bars are unique. The whole is a truly magnificent and immensely important part of fortified Yorkshire's heritage.

The walls we see today date from 1250, although a lot of the stonework results from 19th and 20th-century renovation. But there are Roman walls, including the Multangular Tower featured earlier, and Norman fortifications. They originally completely enclosed the city on both sides of the River Ouse apart from a stretch between Layerthorpe Bridge and the Red Tower where there was the King's Fishpond – a sort of moat – until the River Foss was canalised in 1792. Chains were put across the Ouse at Lendal

and Skeldergate for additional security.

The walls have a host of gates or bars and posterns and an assortment of 39 towers. They were breached in two places near the existing railway station to admit trains to the first York rail terminus.

Going anti-clockwise from the river, the main towers are Lendal, North Street Postern or Barker, Toft's, a sandstone tower by the river near Baile Hill Castle, Davy, Fishergate Postern, Red Tower (so named because it was built of brick in 1490) and the Anglian and Multangular Towers on the Roman stretch. The bars are: Micklegate (where by tradition the Lord Mayor greets the monarch), Victoria, Fishergate, Walmgate, Monk and Bootham which stands on the site of the porta principalis dextra of the Roman fortress.

Walmgate Bar

When it comes to illustrating York's gates and bars, you are spoiled for choice. But, if – as it is – it is necessary to be selective, then Walmgate must have it. Mind you, it was a close run thing in the early 19th century. There was pressure to remove the ancient gateways designed to keep invaders out but not for the convenience of traders wishing to enter. The city fathers also saw brass in their stone but conservationists eventually won the day.

Walmgate emerged from the threatened vandalism by the civic philistines in best condition. It is the most complete of the city's bars with even its 14th-century barbican intact. The portcullis, the 15th-century oak gates of the inner arch and the wicket door are all preserved. The three-storey fortress in magnesian limestone was first mentioned in the 12th century. Five hundred years later it was in the wars and had to be heavily restored after damage in the Civil War siege of 1645-6.

On the inner side it also has a touch of the bizarre – a 16th-century flourish of a wood and plaster two-storey house standing on two Tuscan columns with a timber balcony and balustrade. It is one of the oddities of fortified Yorkshire.

Beverley North Bar

Unlike York, Beverley, one of the glories of English county towns, has no walls. By the 13th century, its prosperity – and it was one of the most prosperous medieval towns because of the wool trade – was protected by a ditch and palisade and four gates. Only one gate remains. It is the North Bar, the earliest English town gate built of brick. It was re-built in 1409 of 125,000 small, irregularly sized, dark brown bricks. They got their colour from local clays. Beverley and Hull (where an estimated 4.7m bricks went into the building of its long-since demolished city walls) pioneered brickmaking in Britain as a result of their close connections with Holland where brickmaking was well established in the 12th century.

The two-storey North Bar has a room over the rib-vaulted archway. Both its faces have small windows, niches for statues, heraldic shields and decorative brickwork below the elaborately crenellated parapet.

It was presumably regarded as a useful defence, otherwise it would not have been rebuilt just before Henry V became an epic king. It was certainly useful in stopping one man from getting out. The story goes that Sir John Hotham, treacherous governor of Hull, was riding for his life to his fortified house only to find 8,000 Parliamentarians in the way in Beverley marketplace. He tried to con them into following him but their colonel had had news of his treachery and tried to arrest him. Hotham promptly galloped for the North Bar only to find it closed against him.

The Bayle, Bridlington

One of the wealthiest monastic houses in Yorkshire was Bridlington Priory, founded by the Augustinians at the beginning of the 12th century. It became a place of pilgrimage when John of Thwing was canonized in 1401. Henry V was among the early pilgrims and passed through one of the only two bits of the priory to survive the vandalism of the Dissolution – a magnificently preserved gatehouse called the Bayle.

I could have chosen the beautiful ruined gatehouse of Kirkham Priory, south west of Malton, to illustrate the defensive nature of some religious houses. But Bridlington's Bayle deserves the accolade. It has been kept in a remarkable state of repair since a licence to crenellate was granted in 1388. A great deal of work on the fabric was done in the 17th and 19th century. It is broad and imposing in ashlar sandstone and has a pointed arch with a vaulted roof and a carriage and pedestrian entrances on the inside.

An original spiral stone staircase leads up to the hall where the prior held his courts. It has subsequently been used as a prison for sailors captured during the Civil War, a meeting place for non-conformists at the time of Charles II, a lodging for soldiers in Napoleon's day, a school and a magistrates' court. It is now a museum.

St Gregory's Church, Bedale

The church can look pretty militant in Yorkshire. You might never confuse the role of their buildings but their castellated architecture can make them seem as if they are ready to go marching as to war. If castle-style churches are not quite two-a-penny, they are not exactly scarce as Yarm, Hubberholme, Kirkby Malham, Kirby Moorside and Goodmanham, testify, to name but a few.

Churches also offered sanctuary. Indeed, the shrine of St John of Beverley (canonized 1037) became one of the most important sanctuaries in England, covering the whole town and not just the precincts of the Minister. But they didn't need to put on military airs and graces — and ramparts — to provide that. It is, however, not every day that you come across a church built like a tower house, with the defence and safety of its parishioners in mind.

Yet that is what we find at Bedale, just off the A1 in North Yorkshire, and at Leathley where the Washburn valley joins the Wharfe near Otley. Both were built to the glory of God and the confusion of Scottish raiders. The tower of St Oswald's at Leathley seems to have been added on to a Norman church for this purpose. St Gregory's (pictured right) dominates the north end of Bedale. Its great solid tower is reputed to have been built after the battle of Bannockburn in 1314. It has a porch leading into a vaulted basement. The three upper stages with small windows are topped by a 15th-century tower. The entrance to the tower proper was guarded by a portcullis to keep the people safe from the tartan horde.

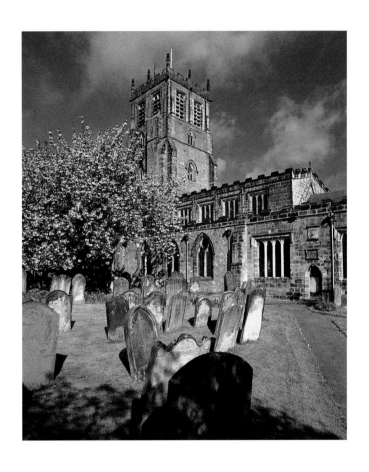

Skelton

There are plenty of castles in Yorkshire, with their castellated walls and turrets, which do not qualify for this book. They are sham in the sense that their purpose was not defensive but nostalgic, indulgent and conceivably self-aggrandising. The present privately owned "castle" at Skelton in Cleveland, between Guisborough and Saltburn, has no place here however attractive it may be at the tip of a diamond-shaped area of more than five acres, surrounded by an 18th-century moat 240ft wide. It was erected from 1794 and its castellated south front is by the Durham architect, Ignatius Bonomi.

But Skelton deserves its place in this book because it once had a formidable castle on this site. The Bruces built a Norman castle there in 1140. It was held by the Fauconbergs for 150 years through six reigns and was one of the great strongholds of the North. Other great families associated with it were the Nevilles and Conyers. It was inherited in ruins by an eccentric hedonist, John Hall Stevenson, an intimate of Laurence Sterne, in the 18th century. He devoted his life to spending his money but not so much on what came to be known as his "Crazy Castle" but on stables designed by Sir John Soane. The remains of the castle were torn down soon after his death in 1785 but a great deal of medieval remains can be found in today's building.

Upsall

Looking at today's Upsall Castle (as it is described), three miles north east of Thirsk, nobody would believe it goes back a long way. It doesn't. It was built only 76 years ago after the previous "castle" – built from 1872 – had burned down in 1918. So what, you may ask, am I doing putting it in this book? Well, it's not to illustrate a sham castle or the British attachment over the centuries to castle architecture.

Instead, Upsall appears here because it has a long history as a castle. Records show that it was one of the 18 Yorkshire castles on which major construction work took place during the 14th century. That was carried out by the Scropes, of Bolton Castle. If there is any truth in one of the tall tales about it, their first castle fell into ruin. A Scrope who came into his forlorn inheritance, dreamt that if he stood on London Bridge he would find enough money to re-build it. So,

dressed as a beggar, he lingered for three days around London Bridge before a tinker told him "If only I could get to Yorkshire, I would soon be rich." "What do you mean?" asked Scrope. "I would find gold under an elder tree at Upsall Castle," replied the tinker. Scrope hurried home and promptly found the wherewithal to build another castle.

It was in ruins when Dr John Turton, Physician in Ordinary to George III, bought the estate in 1772. Captain Edmund Turton began in 1857 to create a magnificent new family seat. The designs for his castle were published in *The Builder* in 1873. This building burned down in 1918 while the owner was preaching in church. By the time Thirsk fire brigade arrived, all was lost. They had been unable to catch the horse to pull the tender.

Castle Howard

As a feeling of greater security spread across the nation following the Civil War, the gentry's mind was not on castles which had, in any case, had their military day. Their growing prosperity led them into more sophisticated architecture. They may have called the results castles but they looked like palaces. Castle Howard on the Howardian Hills south west of Malton is the ultimate legacy in Yorkshire of this spectacular 18th-century expression of confidence in the future.

Charles Howard, the 3rd Earl of Carlisle, decided to rebuild Hinderskelfe Castle, which Leland, in Henry VIII's day, had described as "a fair quadrant of stone having four towers built castle like but it is no ample thing." Thank God, Howard didn't get very far with the Comptroller of His Majesty's Works. Instead, he appointed his fellow member of the Kit Kat Club, John Vanbrugh, who designed the spectacular baroque country estate we see today. They could not have filmed *Brideshead Revisited* anywhere else.

Of course, the age of the castle was not quite dead. Castle Howard is set within a sham rampart with eleven towers. But the castle became a thing of beauty. And to its vast legacy of military and religious construction was added a new and glorious chapter in Yorkshire's architecture. But that is another story.

Photographic credits